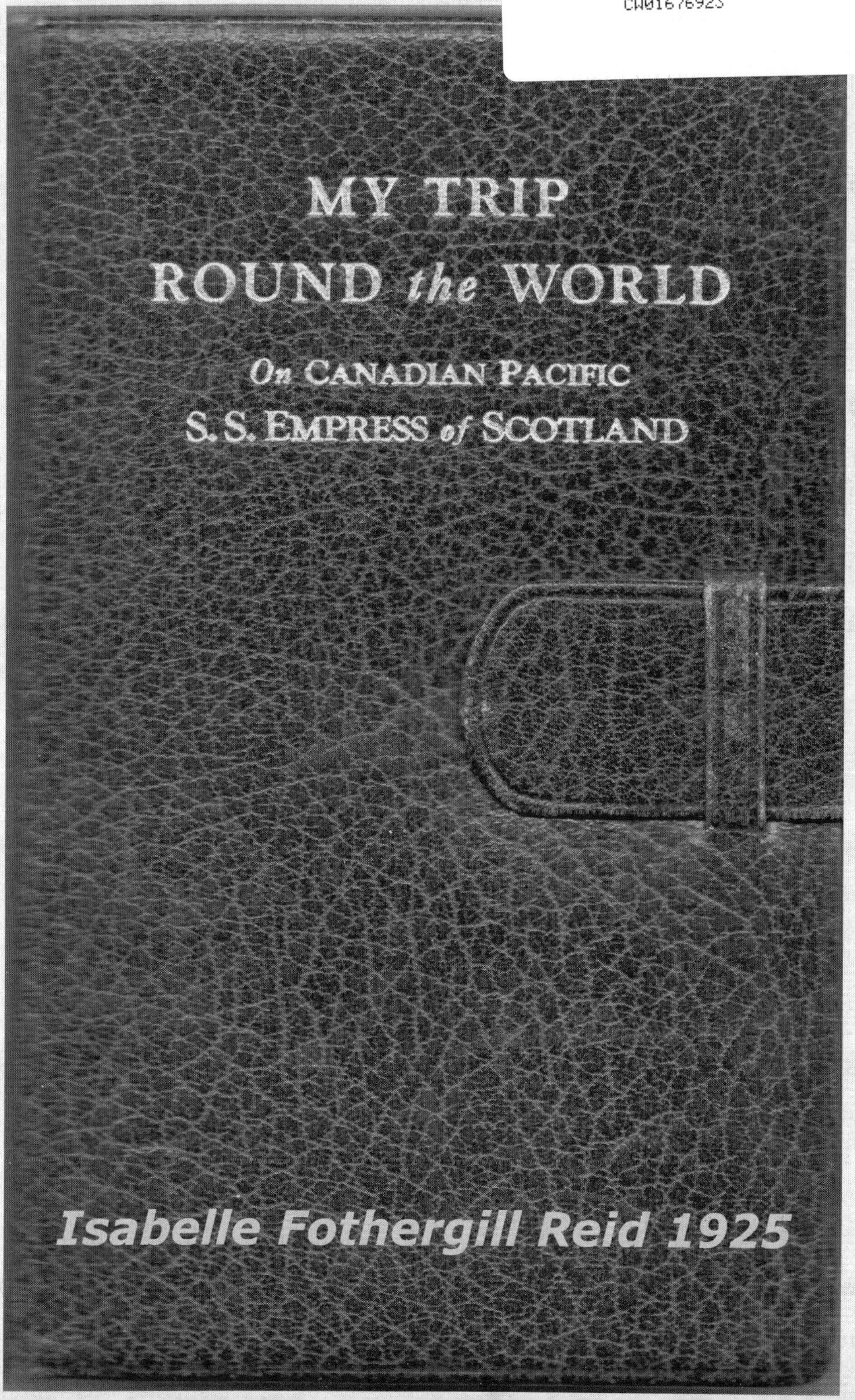
MY TRIP
ROUND the WORLD
On CANADIAN PACIFIC
S. S. EMPRESS of SCOTLAND
Isabelle Fothergill Reid 1925

INTRODUCTION

On November 14th 1925, my mother, Isabelle Fothergill Reid of 23 Hanover House, Regents Park, London N.W.8, together with her mother, Marion Reid, embarked on a 'Round the World' trip aboard Canadian Pacific S.S. Empress of Scotland.

The duration of the tour lasted five and a half months, and they visited a good variety of interesting places.

What follows here is a replica of my mother's diary, page by page, giving her account of the trip. Underneath each page, I have transcribed her handwriting into text which is easier to read.

David Anthony Bayne—January 2011

Isabelle Fothergill Reid in 1925

INDEX OF PLACES WHICH SHE VISITED

Round the world cruise November 14, 1925 to April 21, 1926.

S.S.EMPRESS OF SCOTLAND

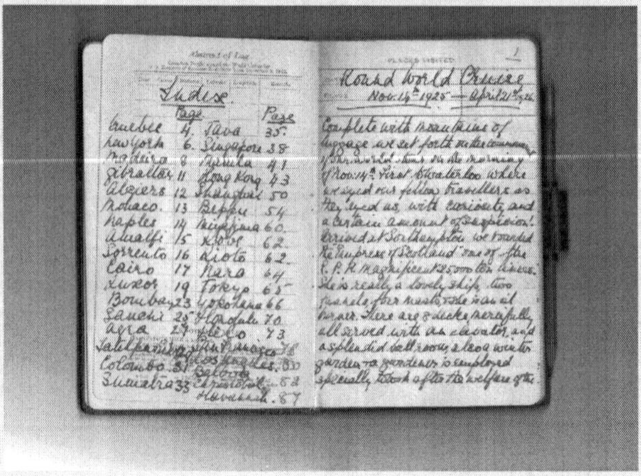

PAGE 1

Complete with mountains of luggage, we set forth for the commencement of our world tour on the morning of November 14th, first to Waterloo where we eyed our fellow travellers as they eyed us with curiosity and a certain amount of suspicion!. We arrived at Southampton where we boarded the Empress of Scotland, one of the Canadian Pacific magnificent 25,000 ton liners. She is really a lovely ship. Two funnels, four masts and she is an oil burner. There are eight decks, mercifully all served with an elevator and a splendid ball-room. Also there is a winter garden and the gardener is employed specially to look after the welfare of the

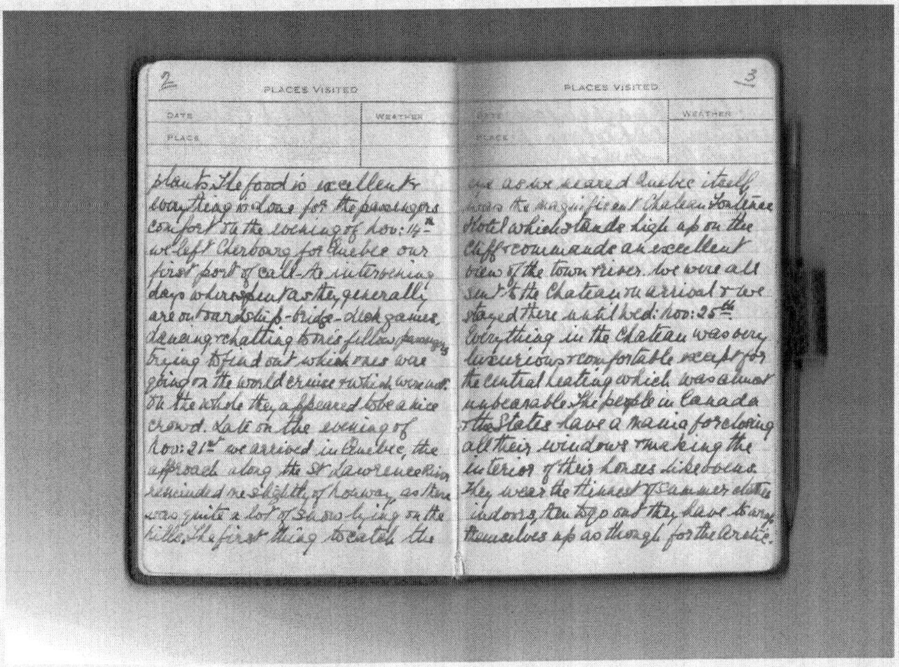

PAGE 2 & 3

plants. The food is excellent and everything is done for the passengers' comfort. On the evening of November 14th, we left Cherbourg for Quebec, our first port of call. The intervening days were spent as they generally are on board ship. Bridge, Deck games, dancing, and chatting to one's fellow passengers trying to find out which ones were going on the world cruise and which were not. On the whole they appeared to be a nice crowd. Late on the evening of November 21st, we arrived in Quebec. The approach along the St Lawrence River reminded me slightly of Norway. There was quite a lot of snow lying on the hills. The first thing to catch the eye as we neared Quebec itself was the magnificent Chateau Fontenaeux Hotel which stands high up on the cliffs and commands an excellent view of the town river. We were all sent to the Chateau on arrival, and we stayed there until Wednesday November 25th. Everything in the Chateau was very luxurious and comfortable except for the central heating which was almost unbearable. The people in Canada and the States have a mania for closing all their windows and making the interior of their houses like ovens. They wear the thinnest of summer clothes indoors, then to go out, they have to wrap themselves up as though for the Arctic.

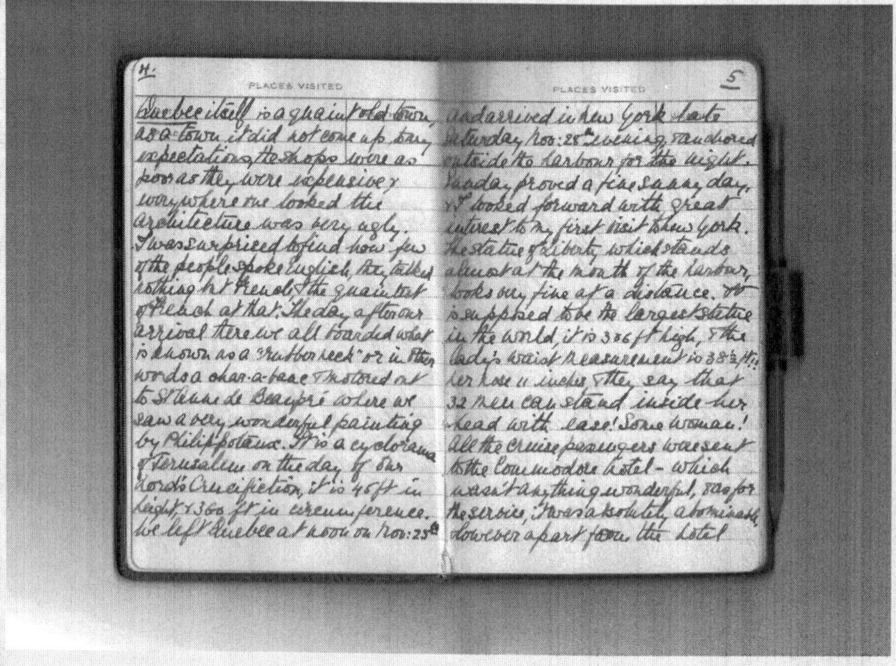

PAGE 4 & 5

Quebec itself is a quaint old town. As a town it did not come up to my expectations. The shops were as poor as they were expensive, and everywhere one looked, the architecture was very ugly. I was surprised to find how few of the people spoke English. They talked nothing but French, the quaintest of French at that. The day after our arrival, we all boarded what is known as a 'rubberneck', or in other words a Charabanc, and motored out to St Anne de Beaupre where we saw a very wonderful painting by Philippotaux. It is a cyclorama of Jerusalem on the day of our Lord's crucifixion. It is 45 feet in height, and 360 feet in circumference. We left Quebec at noon on November 25th, and arrived in New York late on Saturday November 28th in the evening. We anchored outside the harbour for the night. Sunday proved a fine sunny day, and I looked forward with great interest to my first visit to New York. The Statue of Liberty, which stands almost at the mouth of the harbour looked very fine at a distance. It is supposed to be the largest statue in the world. It is 386 feet high, and the lady’s waist measurement is thirty eight and a half feet!. Her nose is 11 inches long, and they say that 32 men can stand inside her head with ease! Some woman! All the cruise passengers were sent to the Commodore Hotel which wasn't anything wonderful. As for the service, it was absolutely abominable, however apart from the hotel

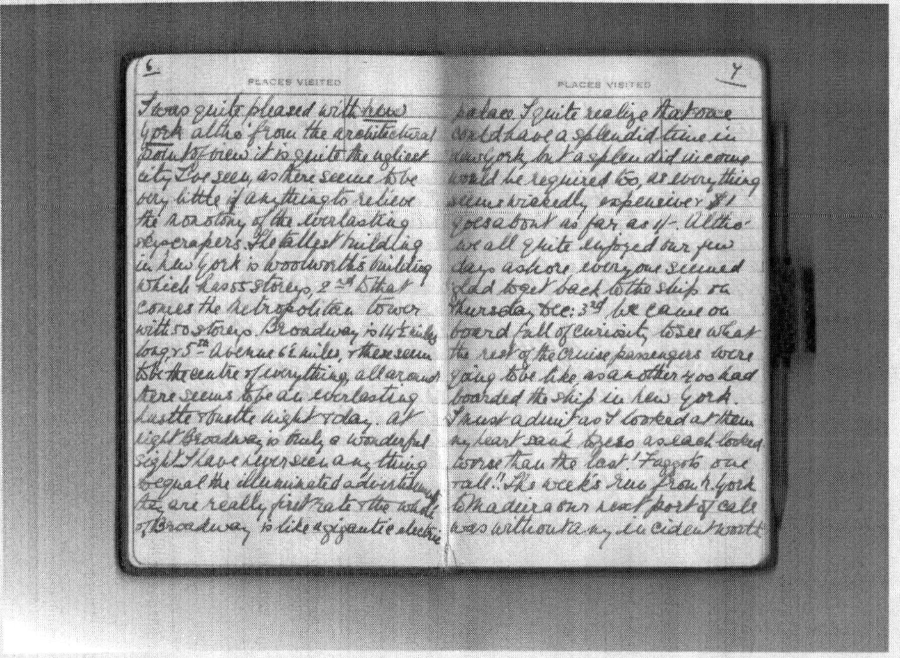

PAGE 6 & 7

I was quite pleased with New York, although from the architectural point of view, it is quite the ugliest city I've seen as there seems to be very little if anything to relieve the monotony of the everlasting skyscrapers. The tallest building in New York is Woolworth's building which has 55 stories. Second to that comes the Metropolitan Tower with 50 stories. Broadway is fourteen and a half miles long and fifth Avenue six and a half miles, and these seem to be the centre of everything. All around there seems to be an everlasting hustle and bustle night and day. At night, Broadway is truly a wonderful sight. I have never seen anything to equal the illuminated advertising, and they are really first rate, and the whole of Broadway is like a gigantic electric palace. I quite realise that one could have a splendid time in New York, but a splendid income would be required too, as everything seems wickedly expensive and one dollar goes about as far as one shilling. Although we all quite enjoyed our few days ashore, everyone seemed glad to get back to the ship. On Thursday December 3rd, we came on board full of curiosity to see what the rest of the cruise passengers were going to be like, as another 400 had boarded the ship in New York. I must admit, as I looked at them my heart sank as each looked worse than the last! Faggots one and all!! The week's run from New York to Madeira, our next port of call was without any incident worth

Chateau Fonteaeux (from page 2 & 3 in the diary

Cyclorama of Jerusalem (page 4 & 5 in the diary)

New York in 1925 (page 6 & 7 in the diary)

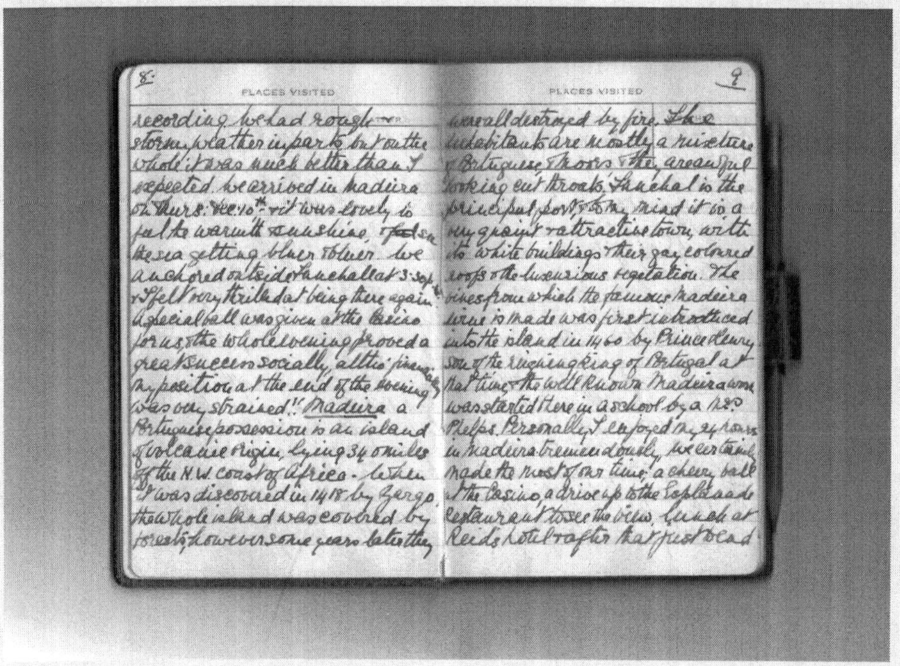

8 PLACES VISITED

recording. We had rough &
stormy weather in parts but on the
whole it was much better than I
expected. We arrived in Madeira
on Thurs: Dec 10th & it was lovely to
feel the warmth & sunshine, & see
the sea getting bluer & bluer. We
anchored outside Funchal at 3:30 p
& I felt very thrilled at being there again
A special ball was given at the Casino
for us, & the whole evening proved a
great success socially, altho' finan-
cially my position at the end of the evening
was very strained!! Madeira a
Portuguese possession is an island
of volcanic origin, lying 340 miles
off the N.W. coast of Africa. When
it was discovered in 1418 by Zargo,
the whole island was covered by
forests, however some years later they

PLACES VISITED 9

were all destroyed by fire. The
inhabitants are mostly a mixture
of Portuguese & Moors & they are awful
looking cut throats. Funchal is the
principal port & to my mind it is a
very quaint & attractive town, with
its white buildings & their gay coloured
roofs & the luxurious vegetation. The
vines from which the famous Madeira
wine is made was first introduced
into the island in 1460 by Prince Henry
son of the reigning King of Portugal at
that time, & the well known Madeira wine
was started there in a school by a Mrs.
Phelps. Personally, I enjoyed my 24 hours
in Madeira tremendously, we certainly
made the most of our time, a cheery ball
at the Casino, a drive up to the Esplanade
restaurant to see the view, lunch at
Reid's Hotel & after that just to end

PAGE 8 & 9

recording. We had rough and stormy weather in parts, but on the whole, it was much better than I expected. We arrived in Madeira on Thursday, December 10th, and it was lovely to feel the warmth and sunshine and see the sea getting bluer and bluer. We anchored outside Funchal at 3:30 pm, and I felt very thrilled at being there again. A special ball was given at the casino for us and the whole evening proved a great success socially, although financially my position at the end of the evening was very strained! Madeira, a Portuguese possession, is an island of volcanic origin lying 340 miles off the north-west coast of Africa. When it was discovered in 1419 by Portuguese sailors, the whole island was covered by forests, however some years later they were all destroyed by fire. The inhabitants are mostly a mixture of Portuguese and moors, and they are awful looking cut throats. Funchal is the principal, and to my mind it is a very quaint and attractive town with its white buildings and their gay coloured roofs and the luxurious vegetation. The vines from which the famous Madeira wine is made was first introduced into the island in 1460 by Prince Henry, son of the reigning king of Portugal at that time, and the well known Madeira wine was started there in a school by a Mrs Phelps. Personally, I enjoyed my 24 hours in Madeira tremendously, and we certainly made the most of our time. A cheery ball at the casino, a drive up to the Esplanade restaurant to see the view, then lunch at Reid's Hotel after that just to end

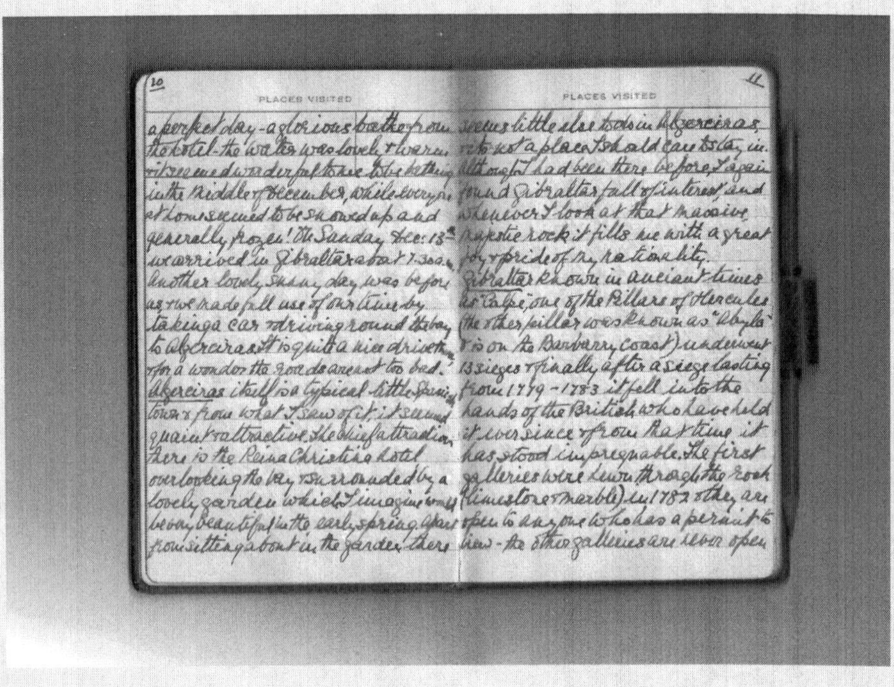

PAGE 10 & 11

a perfect day - a glorious bathe from the hotel - the water was lovely and warm, and it seemed wonderful to be to be bathing in the middle of December while everyone at home seemed to be snowed up and generally frozen! On Sunday, December 13th, we arrived in Gibraltar at 7:30 am. Another lovely sunny day was before us as we made full use of our time by taking a car and driving round the bay to Algeciras. It is quite a nice drive there and for a wonder the roads are not too bad. Algeciras itself is a typical little Spanish town, and from what I saw of it, it seemed quaint and attractive. The chief attraction there is the Reina Christina Hotel overlooking the bay and surrounded by a lovely garden which I imagine would be very beautiful in the early spring. Apart from sitting about in the garden, there seemed little else to do in Algeciras, and it is not a place I should care to stay in. Although I had been there before, I again found Gibraltar full of interest, and whenever I look at that massive majestic rock it fills me with great joy and pride of my nationality. Gibralter, known in ancient times as 'Calpe', one of the pillars of Hercules, (the other pillar was known as 'Abyla' and is on the Barberry Coast), underwent 13 sieges and finally after a siege lasting from 1779 to 1783, it fell into the hands of the British who have held it ever since, and from that time it has stood impregnable. The first galleries were hewn through the rock, (limestone and marble), in 1782 and they are open to anyone who has a permit to view. The other galleries are never open

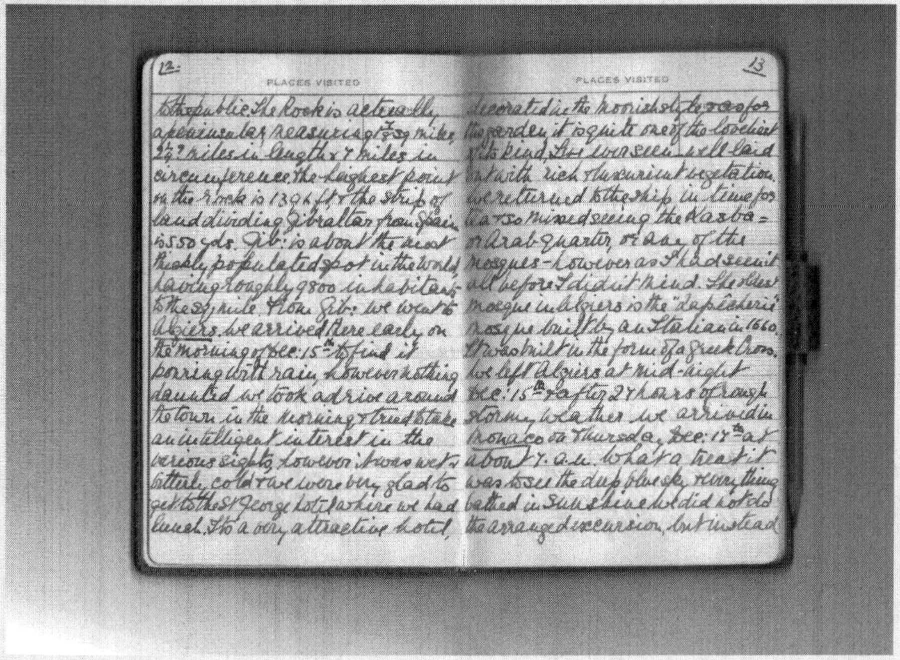

PAGE 12 and 13

to the public. The rock is actually a peninsular measuring 17 mi.², (2 1/4?) miles in the length and 7 miles in circumference. The highest point on the rock is 1396 feet, and the strip of land dividing Gibraltar from Spain is 550 yards. 'Gib is about the most thickly populated spot in the world having roughly 9800 inhabitants to the square mile. From 'Gib, we went to Algiers. We arrived there early in the morning of December 15th to find it pouring with rain, however nothing daunted, we took a drive around the town in the morning, and tried to take an intelligent interest in the various sights, however it was wet and bitterly cold, and we were very glad to get to the St George Hotel where we had lunch. It's a very attractive hotel decorated in the Moorish style, and as for the garden, it is quite one of the loveliest of its kind I'd ever seen - well laid out with rich and luxuriant vegetation. We returned to the ship in time for tea and so missed seeing the kasba or Arab quarter or any of the mosques, however as I had seen it all before I didn't mind. The oldest mosque in Algiers is the 'La Pecherie' mosque built by an Italian in 1660. It was built in the form of a Greek cross. We left Algiers at midnight on December 15th, and after 27 hours of rough stormy weather, we arrived in Monaco on Thursday, December 17th at around 7 am. What a treat it was to see the deep blue sky and everything bathed in sunshine. We did not do the arranged excursion, but instead

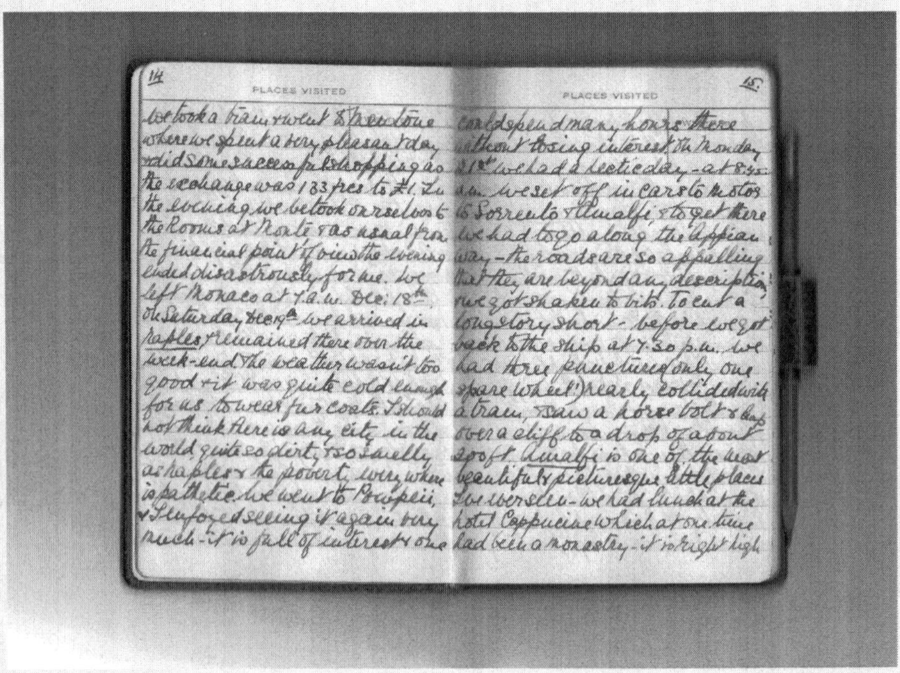
14
PLACES VISITED
we took a tram & went to Mentone
where we spent a very pleasant day
& did some successful shopping as
the exchange was 133 frcs to £1. In
the evening we betook ourselves to
the Rooms at Monte & as usual from
the financial point of view the evening
ended disastrously for me. We
left Monaco at 7 a.m. Dec: 18th.
On Saturday Dec 19th we arrived in
Naples & remained there over the
week-end. The weather wasn't too
good & it was quite cold enough
for us to wear fur coats. I should
not think there is any city in the
world quite so dirty & so smelly
as Naples & the poverty everywhere
is pathetic. We went to Pompeii
& I enjoyed seeing it again very
much - it is full of interest & one

PLACES VISITED
15
could spend many hours there
without losing interest. On Monday
21st we had a hectic day - at 8.45
a.m. we set off in cars to motor
to Sorrento & Amalfi, & to get there
we had to go along the Appian
Way - the roads are so appalling
that they are beyond any description
we got shaken to bits. To cut a
long story short - before we got
back to the ship at 7.30 p.m. we
had three punctures (only one
spare wheel!) nearly collided with
a tram, & saw a horse bolt & leap
over a cliff to a drop of about
200 ft. Amalfi is one of the most
beautiful & picturesque little places
I've ever seen - we had lunch at the
Hotel Cappucine which at one time
had been a monastery - it is right high

PAGE 14 and 15

we took a tram and went to Mentone where we spent a very pleasant day and did some successful shopping as the exchange was 133 Francs to the £1. In the evening we took ourselves to the Rooms at Monte, and as usual from the financial point of view, the evening ended disastrously for me. We left Monaco at 7 am on Dec 18th. On Saturday, December 19th, we arrived in Naples and remained there over the weekend. The weather wasn't too good, and it was quite cold enough for us to wear fur coats. I should not think there is any city in the world quite so dirty and so smelly as Naples, and the poverty everywhere is pathetic. We went to Pompeii, and I enjoyed seeing it again very much. it is full of interest and one could spend many hours there without losing interest. On Monday the 21st, we had a hectic day. at 8:45 am we set off in cars to motor to Sorrento and Amalfi, and to get there we had to go along the Appean Way. The roads are so appalling that they are beyond any description, and we got shaken to bits. To cut a long story short, before we got back to the ship at 7:30 pm, we had three punctures, (only one spare wheel!). We nearly collided with a tram, and saw a horse bolt and leap over a cliff to a drop of about 200 feet. Amalfi is one of the most beautiful and picturesque little places I've ever seen. We had lunch at the Hotel Cappcine which at one time had been a monastery.It is right high

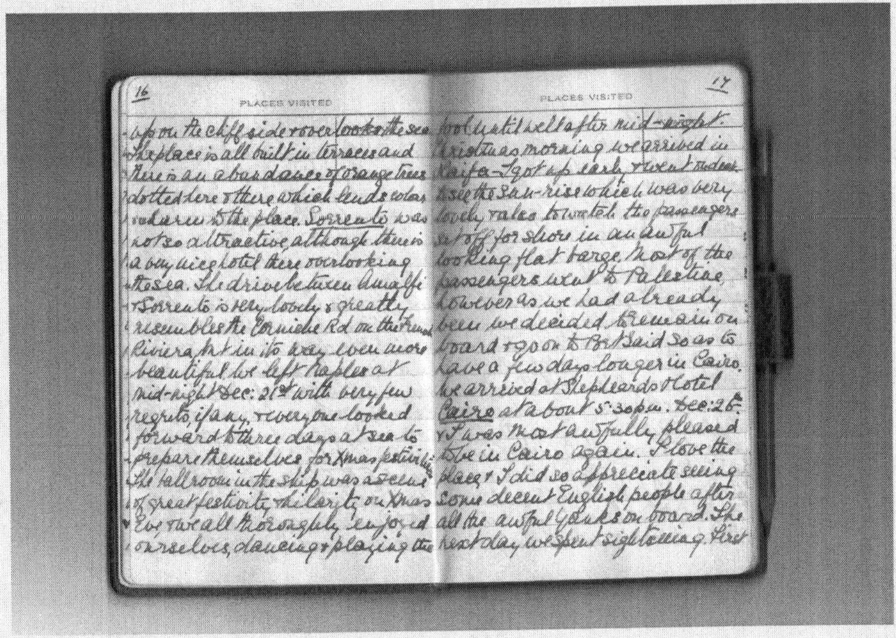

PAGE 16 & 17

up on the cliffside and overlooking the sea. The place is all built in terraces and there is an abundance of orange trees dotted here and there which lends colour and charm to the place. Sorrento was not so attractive, although there is a very nice hotel there overlooking the sea. The drive between Amalfi and Sorrento is very lovely and greatly resembles the Corniche Road on the French Riviera, but in its way even more beautiful. We left Naples at midnight on December 21st with very few regrets if any, and everyone looked forward to three days at sea to prepare themselves for Christmas festivities. The ball-room in the ship was a scene of great festivity and hilarity on Christmas Eve, and we all thoroughly enjoyed ourselves, dancing and playing the fool until well after midnight. On Christmas morning we arrived in Haifa. I got up early and went on deck to see the sunrise which was very lovely, and also to watch the passengers set off for shore in an awful looking flat barge. Most of the pas -sengers went to Palestine, however as we had already been, we decided to remain on board and go to Port Said so as to have a few days longer in Cairo. We arrived at Shepheards Hotel, Cairo at about 5:30 pm on December 26th, and I was most awfully pleased to be in Cairo again. I love the place and I did so appreciate seeing some decent English people after all the awful Yanks on board.The next day we spent sightseeing. First

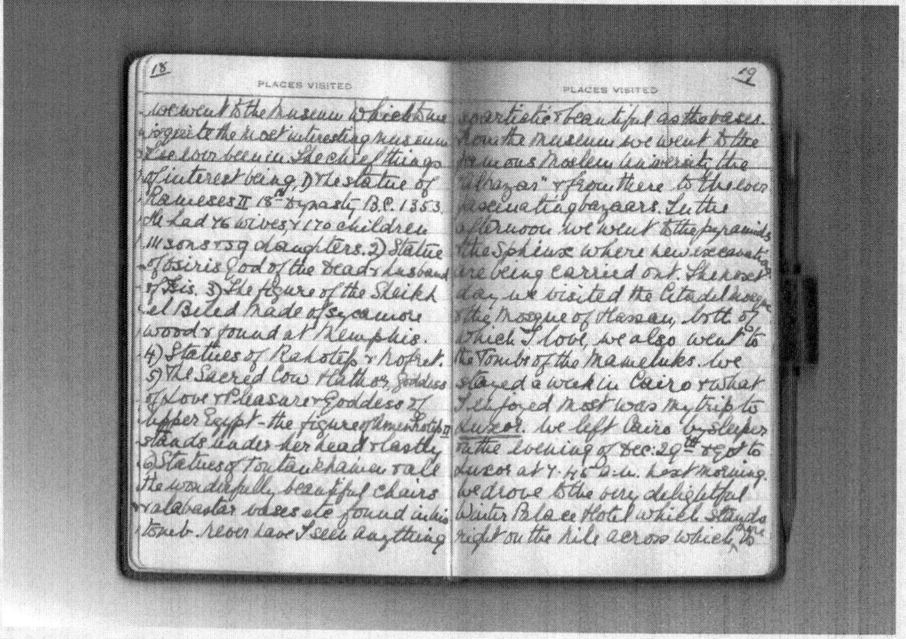

PAGE 18 & 19

we went to the museum which to me is quite the most interesting museum I've ever been in. The chief things of interest being (1) the statue of Ramesses II, 18th Dynasty BC 1353. He had 76 lives and 170 children, 111 sons and 59 daughters. (2) Statue of Osiris, God of the dead and husband of Isis. (3) The figure of the Shiekh of Beled made of sycamore wood and found at Memphis. (4) Statues of Rahotep and Norfret. (5) the Sacred Cow Hathor, Goddess of love and Pleasure and Goddess of Upper Egypt. The figure of Amenholep II stands under her head and lastly, statues of Tutankhamen and all the wonderfully beautiful chairs and alabaster vases etc found in his tomb. Never have I seen anything so artistic and beautiful as the vases. From the museum we went to the famous Moslem University the 'Alhazar', and from there to the ever fascinating bazaars. In the afternoon we went to the Pyramids and the Sphinx where new excavations are being carried out. The next day we visited the Citadel Mosque and the Mosque of Hassau, both of which I love. We also went to the tombs of the Mameluks. We stayed a week in Cairo and what I enjoyed most was my trip to Luxor. We left Cairo by sleeper on the evening of December 29th, and got to Luxor at 7:45 am. Next morning, we drove to the very delightful Winter Palace Hotel which stands right on the hill across which there is

La Percherie Mosque (page 12 & 13 in the diary)

Shepheards Hotel (page 16 & 17 in the diary

Statue of Ramesses II (page 18 & 19 in the diary)

Rahotep and Norfret (page 18 &19 in the diary

Sheikh of Beled (page 18 & 19 in the diary)

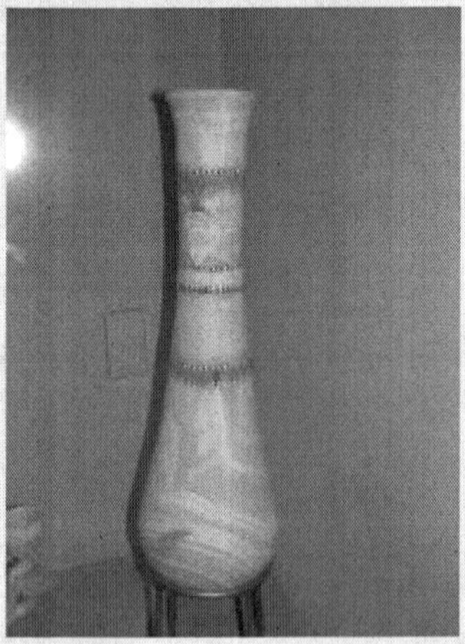

Alabaster vase (page 18 & 19 in the diary)

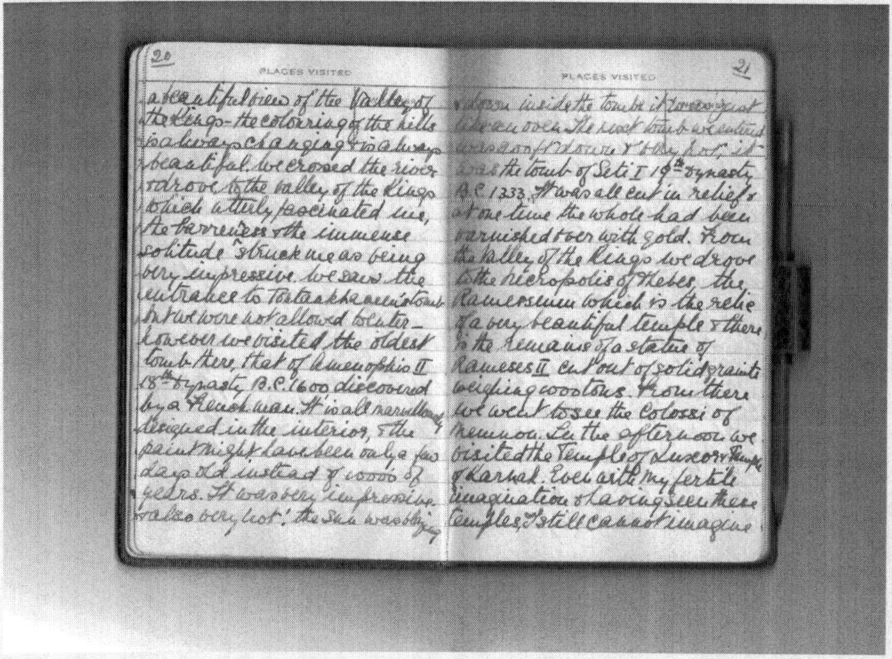

PAGE 20 and 21

a beautiful view of the Valley of the Kings. The Colouring of the hills is always changing and is always beautiful. We crossed the river and drove to the Valley of the Kings which utterly fascinated me, the barrenness and the immense solitude struck me as being very impressive. We saw the entrance to Tutankhamen's tomb but we were not allowed to enter, however we visited the oldest tomb there, that of Amenophis II, 18th Dynasty BC 1600, discovered by a Frenchman. It is all marvellously designed in the interior and the paint might have been only a few days old instead of 10,000 years. It was very impressive, and also very hot. The sun was shining down and inside the tomb it was just like an oven. The next tomb we entered was 200 feet down and very hot. It was the tomb of Seti I,19th Dynasty BC 1333. It was all cut in relief and at one time the whole had been varnished over with gold. From the Valley of the Kings we drove to the Necropolis of Thebes The Ramesseau, which is the relic of a very beautiful temple and there is the remains of a statue of Ramesses II cut out of solid granite weighing 1000 tonnes. From there we went to see the Colossi of Memmon. In the afternoon we visited the temple of Luxor and temple of Karnak. Even with my fertile imagination and having seen these temples, I still cannot imagine

Citadel Mosque (page 18 & 19 in the diary)

Tombs of The Mameluks (page 18 & 19 in the diary

Valley of The Kings (page 20 & 21 in the diary)

Tomb of Amenophis II (page 20 & 21 in the diary)

Tomb of Seti I (page 20 & 21 in the diary)

Necropolis of Thebes (page 20 & 21 in the diary)

Colossi of Memmon (page 20 & 21 in the diary)

Temple of Luxor (page 20 & 21 in the diary)

Temple of Karnak (page 20 & 21 in the diary)

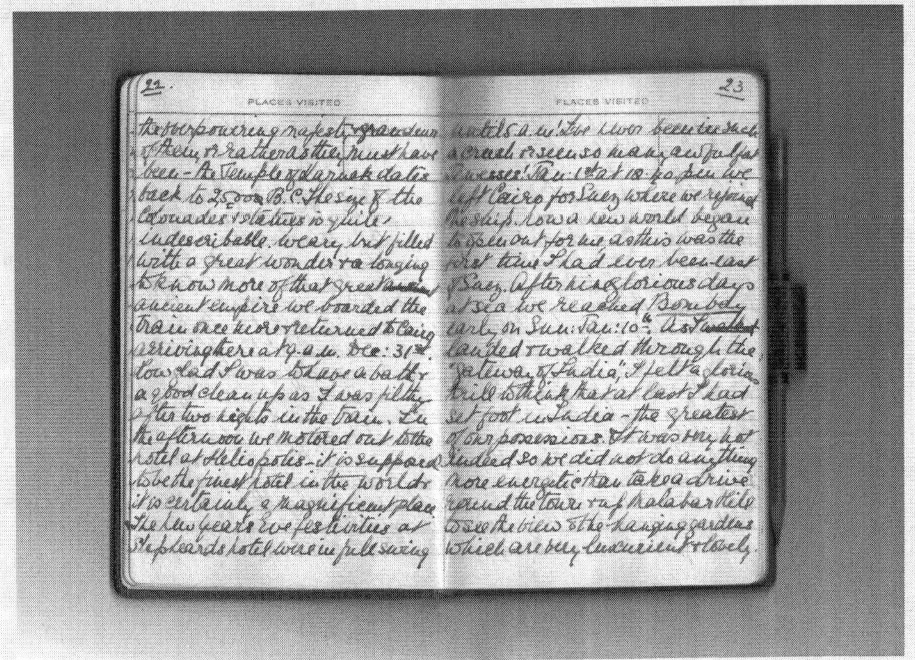

PAGE 22 and 23

the overpowering majesty and grandeur of them, or rather as they must have been. The temple of Karnak dates back to 2500 BC. The size of the colonnades and statues is quite indescribable. Weary, but filled with a great wonder and a longing to know more of that great ancient empire, we boarded the train once more, and returned to Cairo arriving there at 9 am on December 31st. How glad I was to have a bath and a good clean up as I was filthy after two nights in the train. In the afternoon we motored out to the hotel at Heliopolis. It is supposed to be the finest hotel in the world, and is certainly a magnificent place. On New Year's Eve, festivities at Shepheards Hotel were in full swing until 5 am! I've never been in such a crush or seen so many awful Jewesses! On January 1st at 12:40 pm, we left Cairo for Suez where we rejoined the ship. Now a new world began to open out from me, as this was the first time I had ever been east of Suez. After nine glorious days at sea, we reached Bombay early on Sunday January 10th. As I landed and walked through the 'Gateway of India', I felt a glorious thrill to think that at last I had set foot in India, the greatest of our possessions. It was very hot indeed so we did not do anything more energetic than take a drive round the town and up Malabar Hill to see the view of the hanging gardens which are very luxuriant and lovely.

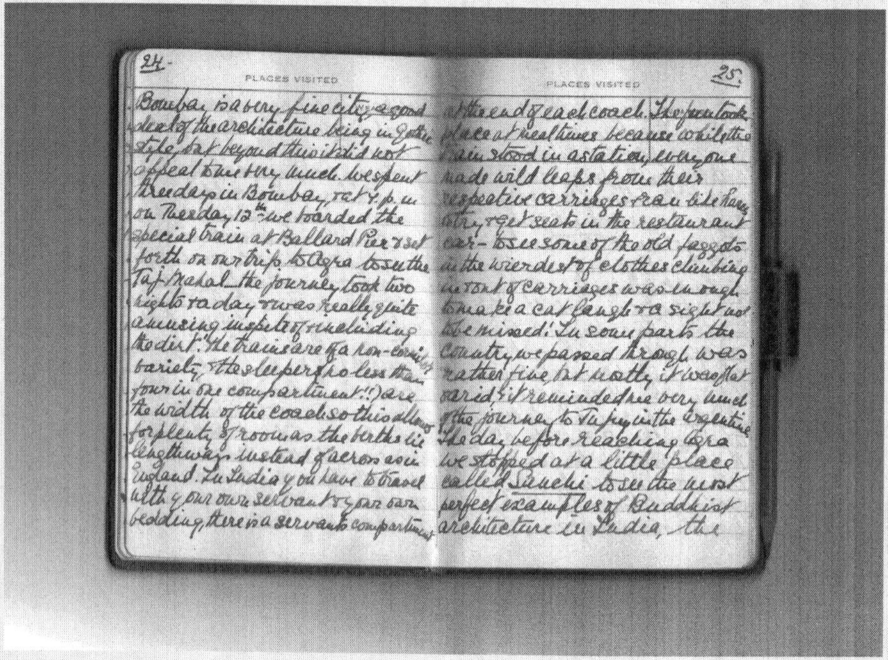

PAGE 24 and 25

Bombay is a very fine city, a good deal of the architecture being in Gothic style, but beyond this it did not appeal to me very much. We spent three days in Bombay, and at 7 pm on Tuesday the 12th, we boarded the special train at Ballard Pier and set forth on our trip to Agra to see the Taj Mahal. The journey took two nights and a day, and was really quite amusing in spite of and including the dirt. The trains are of a non-corridor variety, and the sleepers, (no less than four in one compartment!!), are the width of the coach so this allows for plenty of room as the berths lie lengthways instead of across as in England. In India you have to travel with your own servant and your own bedding. There is a servants compartment at the end of each coach. The fun took place at mealtimes because while the train stood in a station, everyone made wild leaps from their respective carriages and ran like hares to try and get seats in the restaurant car. To see some of the old faggots in the weirdest of clothes climbing in and out of carriages was enough to make a cat laugh, and a sight not to be missed! In some parts, the country we passed through was rather fine, but mostly it was flat acrid, and it reminded me very much of the journey to Jujing in the Argentine. The day before reaching Agra, we stopped at a little place called Sanchi to see the most perfect examples of Buddhist architecture in India, the

Helipolois Hotel 1925 (page 22 & 23 in the diary)

Malabar Hill (page 22 & 23 in the diary)

Taj Mahal (diary page 24 & 25)

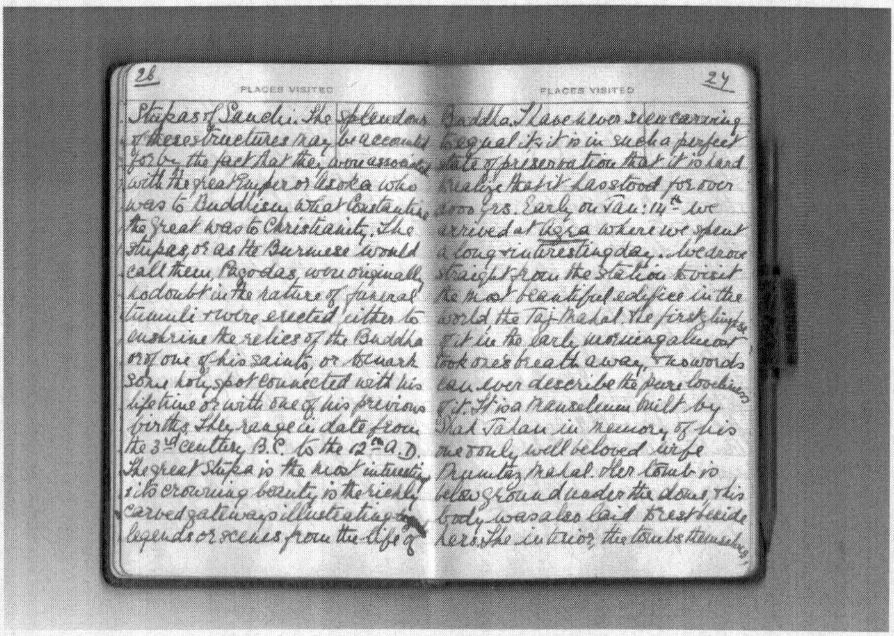

PAGE 26 and 27

Stupas at Sanchi. The splendour of these structures may be accounted for by the fact that they were associated with the great Emperor Ashoka who was to Buddhism what Constantine the Great was to Christianity. The Stupas, or as the Burmese would call them, Pagodas, were originally no doubt in the nature of funeral tumuli and were erected either to enshrine the relics of the Buddha or of one of his saints, or to mark some holy spot connected with his lifetime or with one of his previous births. They range in date from the third century BC to the 12th AD. The great Stupa is the most interesting, and its crowning beauty is the richly carved gateways illustrating legends or scenes from the life of Buddha. I have never seen carving to equal it, and it is in such a perfect state of preservation that it is hard to realise that it has stood for over 2000 years. Early on January 14th, we arrived at Agra where we spent a long and interesting day. We drove straight from the station to visit the most beautiful edifice in the world, The Taj Mahal. The first glimpse of it in the early morning almost took one's breath away, and no words can ever describe the pure loveliness of it. It is a mausoleum built by Shah Jahan in memory of his one and only well beloved wife Mumtaz Mahal. Her tomb is below ground under the dome, and his body was also laid to rest beside hers. The interior, the tombs themselves,

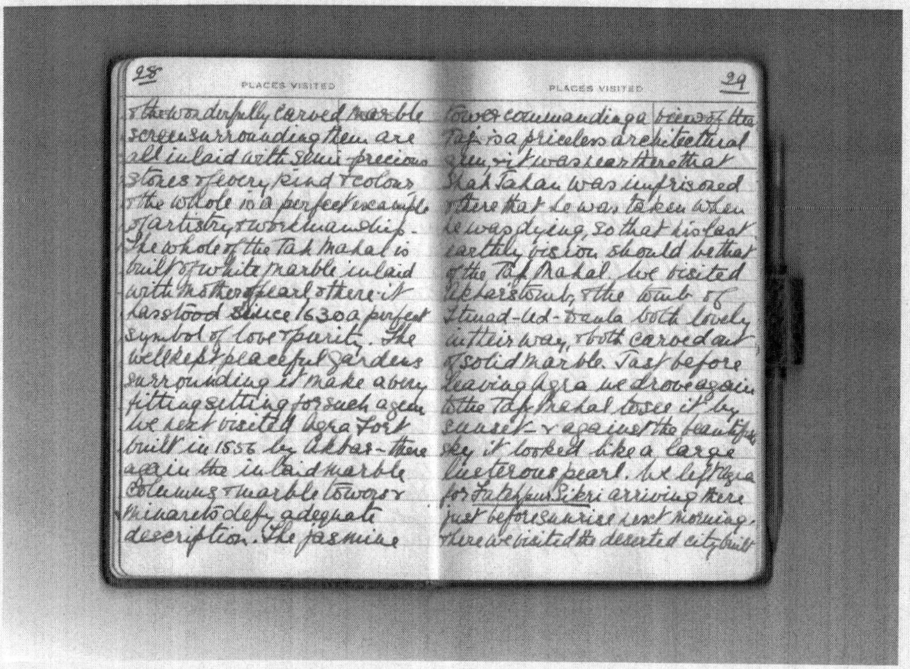

PAGE 28 and 29

and the wonderfully carved marble screen surrounding them are all inlaid with semi-precious stones of every kind and colour, and the whole is a perfect example of artistry and workmanship. The whole of the Taj Mahal is built of white marble inlaid with mother-of-pearl, and there it has stood since 1630, a perfect symbol of love and purity. The well kept peaceful gardens surrounding it make a very fitting setting for such a gem. We next visited Agra Fort built in 1556 by Akbar. There again the inlaid marble columns and marble towers and minarets defy adequate description. The Jasmine Tower, commanding a view of the Taj, is a priceless architectural gem, and it was near there that Shah Jahan was imprisoned, and there that he was taken when he was dying, so that his last earthly vision should be that of the Taj Mahal. We visited Akbar's tomb, and the tomb of Itmad ud Daulah, both lovely in their way and both carved out of solid marble. Just before leaving Agra, we drove again to the Taj Mahal to see it by sunset, and against the beautiful sky, it looked like a large lustrous pearl. We left Agra for Fatehpur Sikri, arriving there just before sunrise next morning. There we visited the deserted city built

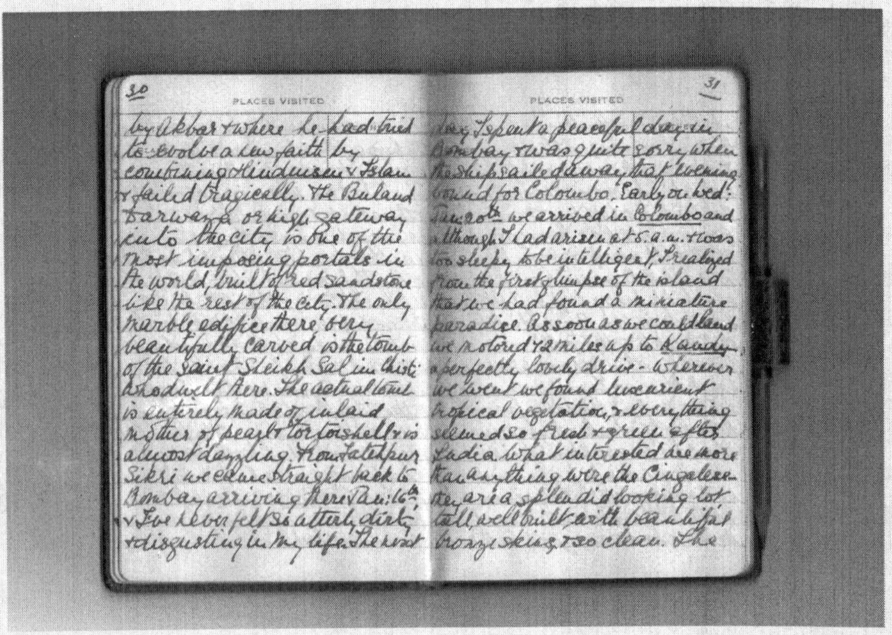

PAGE 30 and 31

by Akbar and where he had tried to evolve a new faith by combining Hinduism and Islam and failed tragically. The Buland Darwasa, or High Gateway into the city is one of the most imposing portals in the world, built of red sandstone like the rest of the city. The only marble edifice there, very beautifully carved, is the tomb of the Saint Sheikh Salim Chiste who dwelt there. The actual tomb is entirely made of inlaid mother of pearl and tortoiseshell, and is almost dazzling. From Fatehpur Sikri we came straight back to Bombay arriving there on January 16th, and I've never felt so utterly dirty and disgusting in my life. The next day I spent a peaceful day in Bombay, and was quite sorry when the ship sailed away that evening bound for Colombo. Early on Wednesday, January 20th, we arrived in Colombo, and although I had arisen at 5 am, I was too sleepy to be intelligent. I realised from the first glimpse of the island that we had found a miniature paradise. As soon as we could land, we motored 72 miles up to Kandy, a perfectly lovely drive. Wherever we went we found luxuriant tropical vegetation, and everything seemed so fresh and green after India. What interested me more than anything were the Singhalese. they are a splendid looking lot. Tall, well built with beautiful bronzed skin, and so clean. The

Stupas at Sanchi (page 26 & 27 in the diary)

The Buland Darwanza (page 30 & 31 in the diary)

Tomb of Saint Sheikh Salim Chiste (page 30 & 31 in the diary)

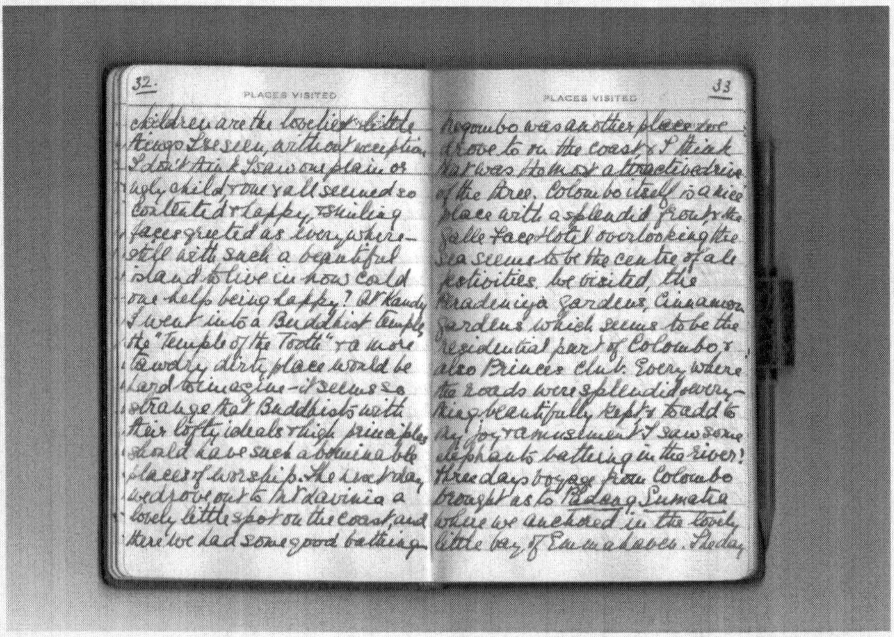

PAGE 32 and 33

children are the loveliest little things I've seen without exception. I don't think I saw one plain or ugly child, and one and all seemed so contented and happy, and smiling faces greeted us everywhere. Still, with such a beautiful island to live in, how could one help being happy?. At Kandy I went into a Buddhist temple, the "Temple of the Tooth", and a more tawdry, dirty place would be hard to imagine. It seems so strange that Buddhists with their lofty ideas and high principles should have such abominable places of worship. The next day we drove out to Mount Lavinia, a lovely little spot on the coast, and there we had some good bathing. Negombo was another place we drove to on the coast, and I think that was the most attractive drive of the three. Colombo itself is a nice place with a splendid front and the Galle Face Hotel overlooking the sea seems to be the centre of all festivities. We visited the Peradeniya Gardens, Cinnamon Gardens which seems to be the residential part of Columbo, and also Princes Club. Everywhere the roads were splendid and everything beautifully kept, and to add to my joy and amusement, I saw some elephants bathing in the river! Three days voyage from Colombo brought us to Padang, Sumatra, where we anchored in the lovely little bay of Emmahaven. The day

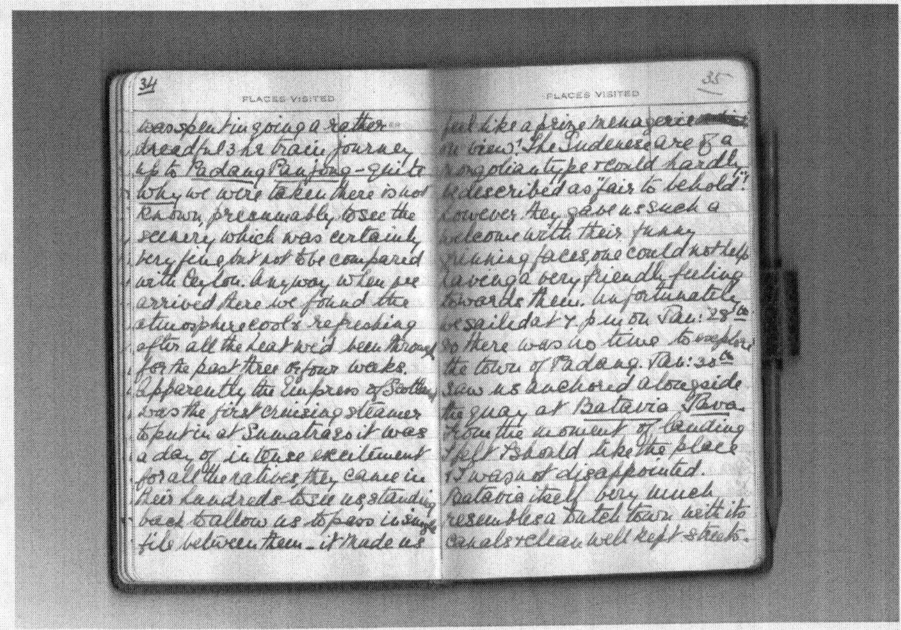

PAGE 34 and 35

was spent in going a rather dreadful three hour train journey up to Padang and Panjong. Quite why we were taken there is not known, presumably to see the scenery which was certainly very fine, but not to be compared with Ceylon. Anyway, when we arrived there we found the atmosphere cool and refreshing after all the heat we'd been through for the past three or four weeks. Apparently the Empress of Scotland was the first cruising steamer to put in at Sumatra, so it was a day of intense excitement for all the natives. They came in their hundreds to see us, standing back to allow us to pass in single file between them. It made us feel like a prize menagerie on view! The Sudanese are of a Mongolian type, and could hardly be described as "fair to behold"! However, they gave us such a welcome with their funny grinning faces, one could not help having a very friendly feeling towards them. Unfortunately we sailed at 7 pm on January 28th, so there was no time to explore the town of Padang. January 30th saw us anchored alongside the quay at Batvia, Java. From the moment of landing I felt I should like the place and I was not disappointed. Batvia itself very much resembles a Dutch town with its canals and clean well kept streets.

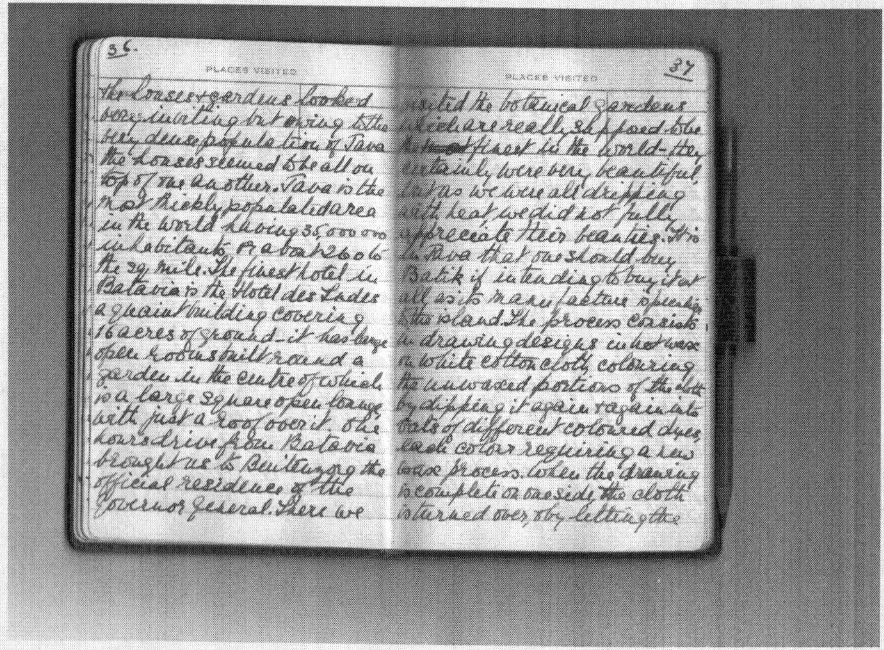
36.

PLACES VISITED

the houses & gardens looked
very inviting but owing to the
very dense population of Java
the houses seemed to be all on
top of one another. Java is the
most thickly populated area
in the world having 35,000,000
inhabitants or about 260 to
the sq. mile. The finest hotel in
Batavia is the Hotel des Indes
a quaint building covering
16 acres of ground - it has large
open rooms built round a
garden in the centre of which
is a large square open lounge
with just a roof over it. One
hours drive from Batavia
brought us to Buitenzorg the
official residence of the
Governor General. There we

PLACES VISITED

37

visited the botanical gardens
which are really supposed to be
the finest in the world - they
certainly were very beautiful
but as we were all dripping
with heat we did not fully
appreciate their beauties. It is
in Java that one should buy
Batik if intending to buy it at
all as its manufacture is peculiar
to the island. The process consists
in drawing designs in hot wax
on white cotton cloth, colouring
the unwaxed portions of the cloth
by dipping it again & again into
vats of different coloured dyes
each colour requiring a new
wax process. When the drawing
is complete on one side the cloth
is turned over, & by letting the

PAGE 36 and 37

The houses and gardens looked very inviting, but owing to the very dense population of Java, the houses seemed to be all on top of one another. Java is the most thickly populated area in the world having 35 million inhabitants, or about 260 to the square mile. The finest hotel in Batvia is the Hotel des Indes, a quaint building covering 16 acres of ground. it has large open rooms built round a garden in the centre of which is a large square open lounge with just a roof over it. One hour's drive from Batvia brought us to Buitenzorg, the official residence of the Governor General. There we visited the Botanical Gardens which are really supposed to be the finest in the world. They cer-tainly were very beautiful, but as we were all dripping with heat, we did not fully appreciate their beauties. It is in Java that one should buy Batik, if in-tending to buy it at all, as its manufacture is peculiar to the island. The proc-ess consists of drawing designs in hot wax on white cotton cloth, colouring the unwaxed portions of the cloth by dipping it again and again into vats of differ-ent col-oured dyes, each colour requiring a new wax process. When the draw-ing is complete on one side, the cloth is turned over, and by letting the

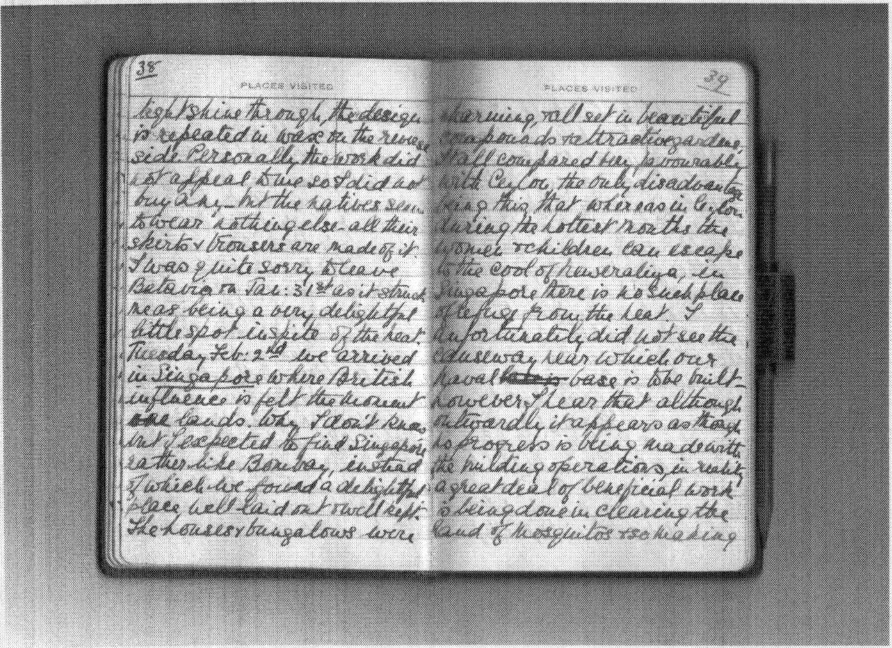

PAGE 38 and 39

light shine through the design, is repeated in wax on the reverse side. Personally, the work did not appeal to me so I did not buy any, but the natives seem to wear nothing else. All their skirts and trousers are made of it. I was quite sorry to leave Batvia on January 31 as it struck me as being a very delightful little spot in spite of the heat. On Tuesday, February 2nd, we arrived in Singapore where British influence is felt the moment one lands. Why, I don't know, but I expected to find Singapore rather like Bombay, instead of which we found a delightful place well laid out and well kept. The houses and bungalows were charming, and all set in beautiful compounds and attractive gardens. It all compared very favourably with Ceylon, the only disadvantage being that whereas in Ceylon during the hottest months, the women and children can escape to the cool of Nuwara Eliya, and in Singapore there is no such place of refuge from the heat. I unfortunately did not see the causeway near which our Naval base is to be built, however I hear that although outwardly it appears as though no progress is being made with the building operations, in reality a great deal of beneficial work is being done in clearing the land of mosquitos and so making

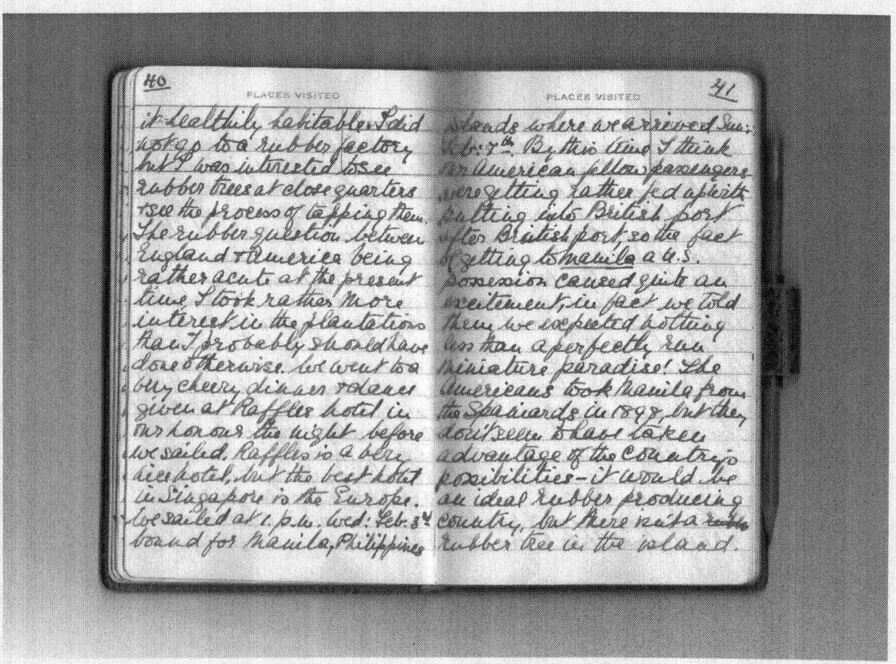

PAGE 40 and 41

it healthily habitable. I did not go to a rubber factory, but I was interested to see rubber trees at close quarters and see the process of tapping them. The rubber question between England and America being rather acute at the present time, I took rather more interest in the plantations than I probably should have done otherwise. We went to a very cheery dinner and dance given at Raffles Hotel in our honour the night before we sailed. Raffles is a very nice hotel, but the best hotel in Singapore is The Europa. We sailed at 1 pm on Wednesday, February 3rd, bound for Manila, Philippines Islands, where we arrived on Sunday, February 7th. By this time I think our American fellow passengers were getting rather fed up with putting into British port after British port, so the fact of getting to Manila, a US possession caused quite an excitement. In fact we told them we expected nothing less than a perfectly run miniature paradise! The Americans took Manila from the Spaniards in 1898, but they don't seem to have taken advantage of the country's possibilities. It would be an ideal rubber producing country, but there isn't a rubber tree in the island.

Galle Face Hotel (page 32 & 33 in the diary)

Hotel des Indes (page 36 & 37 in the diary)

Raffles in 1925 (page 40 & 41 in the diary)

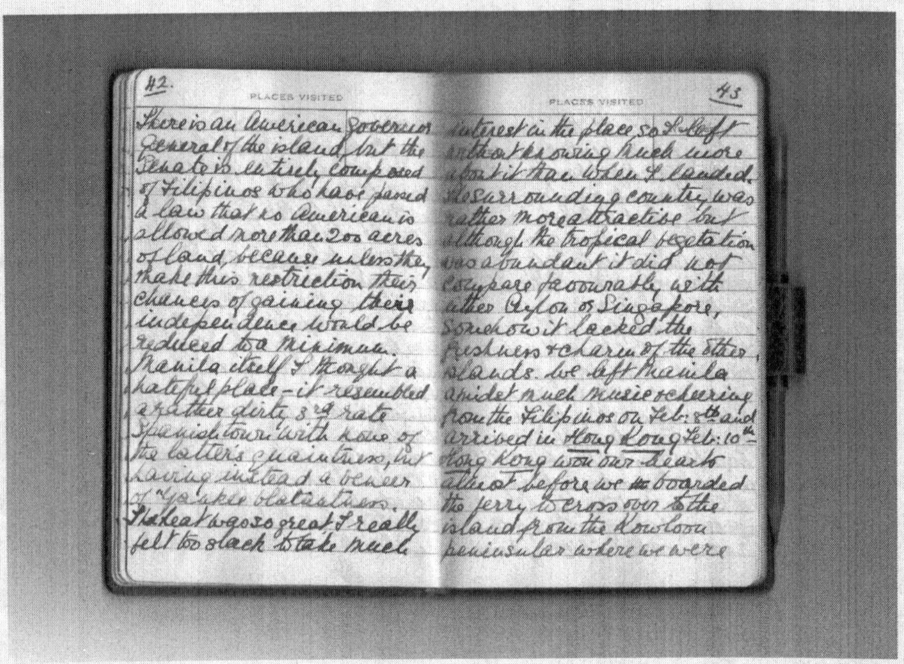

42. PLACES VISITED

There is an American governor
General of the island, but the
Senate is entirely composed
of Filipinos who have passed
a law that no American is
allowed more than 200 acres
of land, because unless they
make this restriction their
chances of gaining their
independence would be
reduced to a minimum.
Manila itself I thought a
hateful place - it resembled
a rather dirty 3rd rate
Spanish town with none of
the latter's quaintness, but
having instead a veneer
of "Yankee blatantness".
The heat was so great I really
felt too slack to take much

PLACES VISITED 43.

interest in the place, so I left
without knowing much more
about it than when I landed.
The surrounding country was
rather more attractive but
although the tropical vegetation
was abundant it did not
compare favourably with
either Ceylon or Singapore,
Somehow it lacked the
freshness & charm of the other
islands. We left Manila
amidst much music & cheering
from the Filipinos on Feb: 8th and
arrived in Hong Kong Feb: 10th.
Hong Kong won our hearts
almost before we boarded
the ferry to cross over to the
island from the Kowloon
peninsular where we were

PAGE 42 and 43

There is an American governor general of the island, but the Senate is entirely composed of Filipinos who have passed a law that no American is allowed more than 200 acres of land because unless they make this restriction, their chances of gaining their independence would be reduced to a minimum. Manila itself I thought a hateful place. It resembled a rather dirty third rate Spanish town with none of the latter's quaintness, but having instead a veneer of "Yankee blatentness". The heat was so great, I really felt too slack to take much interest in the place, so I left without knowing much more about it than when I landed. The surrounding country was rather more attractive, but although the tropical vegetation was abundant, it did not compare favourably with either Ceylon or Singapore. Somehow it lacked the freshness and charm of the other islands. We left Manila amidst much music and cheering from the Filipinos on February 8th, and arrived in Hong Kong on February 10th. Hong Kong won our hearts almost before we boarded the ferry to cross over to the island from the Kowloon peninsula where we were

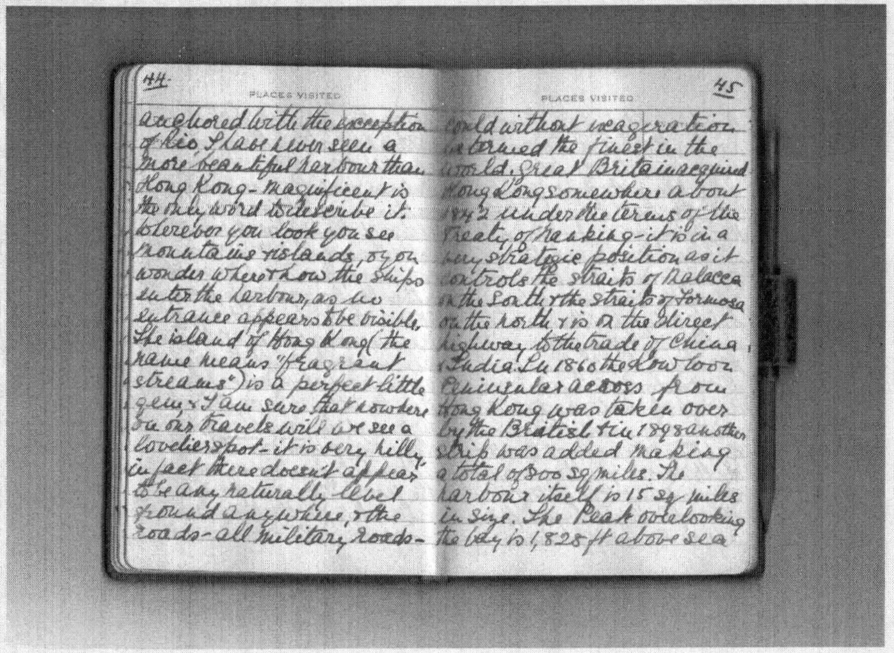

PAGE 44 and 45

anchored. With the exception of Rio, I have never seen a more beautiful harbour than Hong Kong. Magnificent is the only word to describe it. Wherever you look, you see mountains and Islands, and you wonder where and how the ships enter the harbour as no entrance appears to be visible. The island of Hong Kong, the name means "Fragrant Streams", is a perfect little gem, and I am sure that nowhere on our travels will we see a lovelier spot. It is very hilly, in fact there doesn't appear to be any naturally level ground anywhere, and the roads, all military roads, could without exaggeration be termed the finest in the world. Great Britain acquired Hong Kong somewere about 1842 under the terms of the Treaty of Nanking. It is in a very strategic position as it controls the Straits of Malacca on the South and the Straits of Formosa on the North, and is on the direct highway to the trade of China and India. In 1860, the Kowloon Peninsula across from Hong Kong was taken over by the British, and in 1898 another strip was added making a total of 800 square miles. The harbour itself is 15 square miles in size. The peak overlooking the bay is 1828 feet above sea

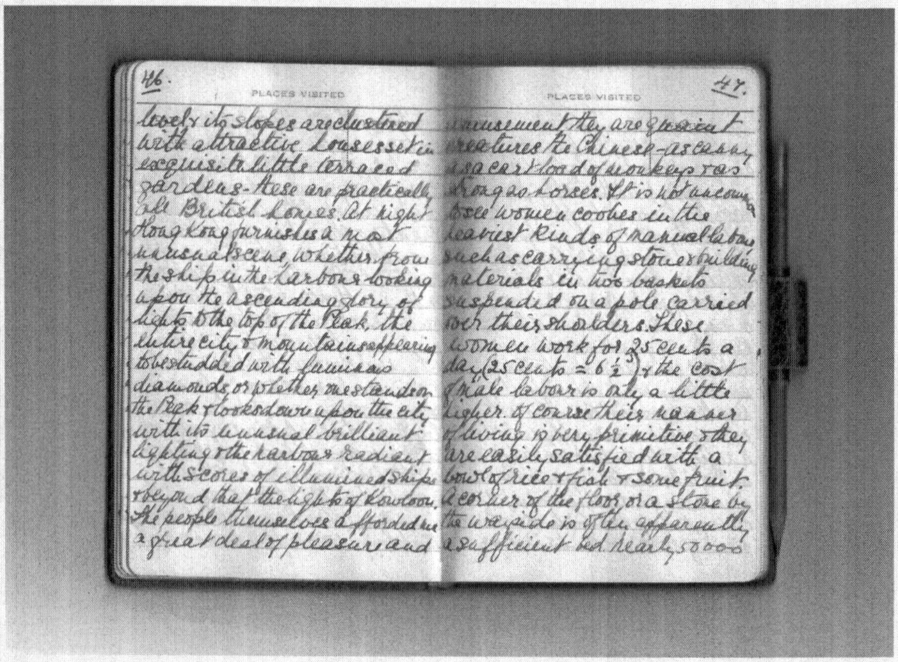

PAGE 46 and 47

level, and its slopes are clustered with attractive houses set in exquisite little terraced gardens. These are practically all British homes. At night, Hong Kong furnishes a most unusual scene, whether from the ships in the harbour looking upon the ascending glory of lights to the top of the peak, the entire city and mountains appearing to be studded with luminous diamonds, or whether one stands on the peak to look down upon the city with its unusual brilliant lighting and the harbour radiant with scores of illuminated ships, and beyond that the lights of Kowloon. The people themselves afforded me a great deal of pleasure and amusement. They are quaint creatures the Chinese, as canny as a cart load of monkeys, and as strong as horses. It is not uncommon to see women coolies in the heaviest kinds of manual labour such as carrying stone and building materials in two baskets suspended on a pole carried over their shoulders. These women work for 25 cents a day, (25 cents equals 6 and a half pennies), and the cost of male labour is only a little higher. Of course their manner of living is very primitive, and they are easily satisfied with a bowl of rice and fish and some fruit. A corner of the floor or a stone by the wayside is often apparently a sufficient bed. Nearly 50,000

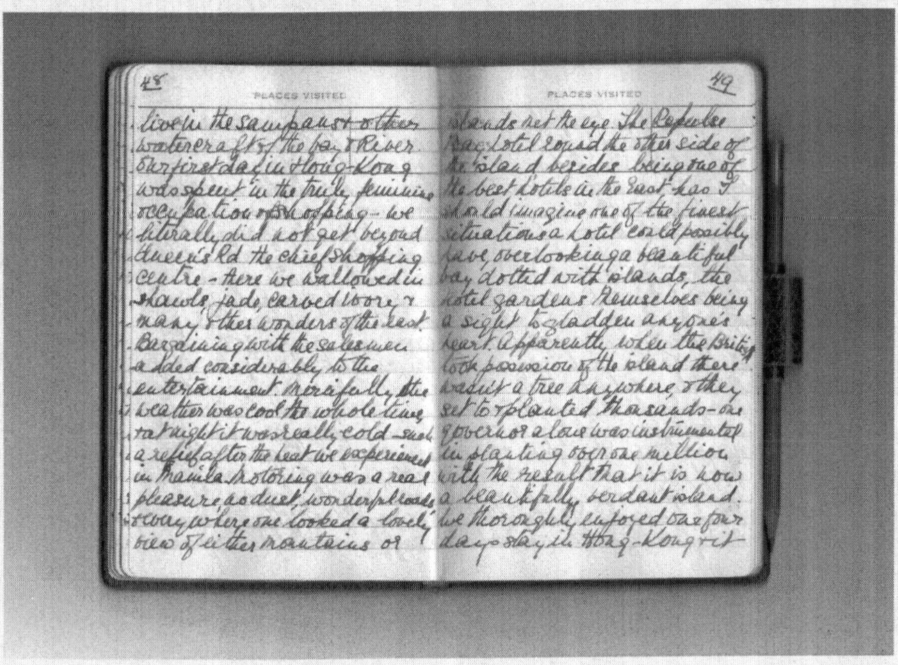
48 PLACES VISITED

live in the sampans & other
watercrafts of the bay & River.
Our first day in Hong-Kong
was spent in the truly feminine
occupation of shopping - we
literally did not get beyond
Queen's Rd the chief shopping
centre - there we wallowed in
shawls, jade, carved ivory &
many other wonders of the East.
Bargaining with the salesmen
added considerably to the
entertainment. Mercifully the
weather was cool the whole time
& at night it was really cold - such
a relief after the heat we experienced
in Manila. Motoring was a real
pleasure, no dust, wonderful roads,
everywhere one looked a lovely
view of either mountains or

PLACES VISITED 49

islands met the eye. The Repulse
Bay Hotel round the other side of
the island besides being one of
the best hotels in the East, has I
should imagine one of the finest
situations a hotel could possibly
have, overlooking a beautiful
bay dotted with islands, the
hotel gardens themselves being
a sight to gladden anyone's
heart. Apparently when the British
took possession of the island there
wasn't a tree anywhere, & they
set to & planted thousands - one
governor alone was instrumental
in planting over one million
with the result that it is now
a beautifully verdant island.
We thoroughly enjoyed our four
days stay in Hong-Kong & it

PAGE 48 and 49

live in the sampans and other watercraft of the bay and river. Our first day in Hong Kong was spent in the truly feminine occupation of shopping. We literally did not get beyond Queens Road, the chief shopping centre. There we wallowed in shawls, jade, carved ivory and many other wonders of the East. Bargaining with the salesmen added considerably to the entertainment. Mercifully, the weather was cool the whole time, and at night it was really cold. Such a relief after the heat we experienced in Manila. Motoring was a real pleasure. No dust, wonderful roads, and everywhere that one looked, a lovely view of either mountains or islands met the eye. The Repulse Bay Hotel, round the other side of the island, besides being one of the best hotels in the East, has I should imagine one of the finest situations a hotel could possibly have, overlooking a beautiful bay dotted with islands. The hotel gardens themselves being a sight to gladden anyone's heart. Apparently, when the Brit-ish took possession of the island, there wasn't a tree anywhere, and they set to and planted thousands. One governor alone was instrumental in planting over 1 million, with the result that it is now a beautifully verdant island. We thoroughly enjoyed our four days stay in Hong Kong and it

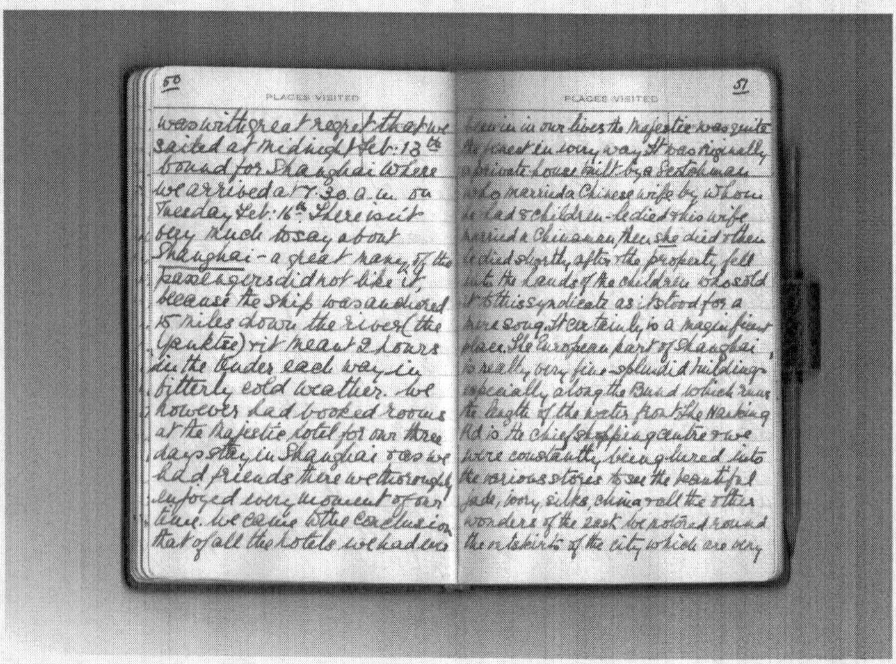
50 PLACES VISITED
was with great regret that we
sailed at midnight Feb. 13th
bound for Shanghai where
we arrived at 7.30 a.m. on
Tuesday Feb. 16th. There isn't
very much to say about
Shanghai - a great many of the
passengers did not like it,
because the ship was anchored
15 miles down the river (the
Yangtse) & it meant 2 hours
in the tender each way in
bitterly cold weather. We
however had booked rooms
at the Majestic Hotel for our three
days stay in Shanghai & as we
had friends there we thoroughly
enjoyed every moment of our
time. We came to the conclusion
that of all the hotels we had ever

PLACES VISITED 51
been in in our lives the Majestic was quite
the finest in every way. It was originally
a private house built by a Scotchman
who married a Chinese wife by whom
he had 8 children - he died & his wife
married a Chinaman, then she died & then
he died shortly after the property fell
into the hands of the children who sold
it to this syndicate as it stood for a
mere song. It certainly is a magnificent
place. The European part of Shanghai,
is really very fine - splendid buildings
especially along the Bund which runs
the length of the water front. The Nanking
Rd is the chief shopping centre & we
were constantly being lured into
the various stores to see the beautiful
jade, ivory, silks, china & all the other
wonders of the east. We motored round
the outskirts of the city which are very

PAGE 50 and 51

was with great regret that we sailed at midnight on February 13th, bound for Shanghai where we arrived at 7:30 am on Tuesday, February 16th. There isn't very much to say about Shanghai. A great many of the passengers did not like it because the ship was anchored 15 miles down the river,(the Yangtse), and it meant two hours in the tender each way in bitterly cold weather. We, however, had booked rooms at the Majestic Hotel for our three days stay in Shanghai, and as we had friends there, we thoroughly enjoyed every moment of our time. We came to the conclusion that of all the hotels we have ever been in in our lives, the Majestic was quite the finest in every way. It was originally a private house built by a Scotsman who married a Chinese wife by whom he had eight children. He died, and his wife married a Chinaman, then she died, and then he died shortly after and the property fell into the hands of the children who sold it to this syndicate as it stood for a mere song. It certainly is a magnificent place. The European part of Shanghai is really very fine with splendid buildings, especially along the Bund, which runs the length of the water front. The Nanking Road is the chief shopping centre, and we were constantly being lured into the various stores to see the beautiful jade, ivory, silks, china and all the other wonders of the East. We motored round the outskirts of the city which are very

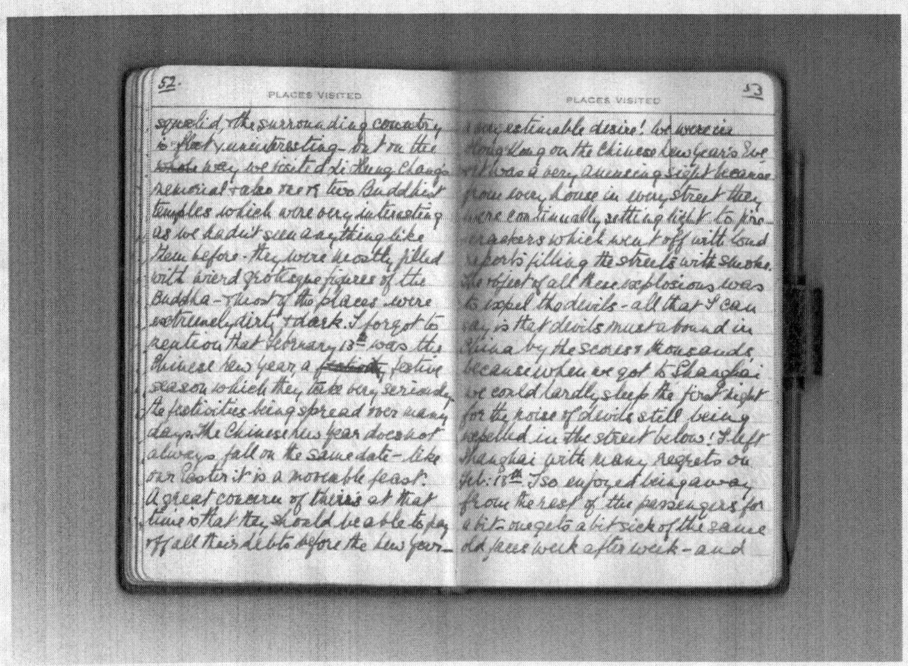
52.

PLACES VISITED

squalid, the surrounding country
is flat & uninteresting - but on the
whole way we visited Li Hung Chang's
memorial & also one or two Buddhist
temples which were very interesting
as we hadn't seen anything like
them before - they were mostly filled
with weird grotesque figures of the
Buddha - most of the places were
extremely dirty & dark. I forgot to
mention that February 13th was the
Chinese New Year, a ~~festivity~~ festive
season which they take very seriously,
the festivities being spread over many
days. The Chinese New Year does not
always fall on the same date - like
our Easter it is a moveable feast.
A great concern of theirs at that
time is that they should be able to pay
off all their debts before the New Year -

PLACES VISITED

53

a very estimable desire! We were in
Hong Kong on the Chinese New Year's Eve
& it was a very amusing sight because
from every house in every street they
were continually setting light to fire-
crackers which went off with loud
reports filling the streets with smoke.
The object of all these explosions was
to expel the devils - all that I can
say is that devils must abound in
China by the scores & thousands,
because when we got to Shanghai
we could hardly sleep the first night
for the noise of devils still being
expelled in the street below! I left
Shanghai with many regrets on
Feb. 18th. I so enjoyed being away
from the rest of the passengers for
a bit - one gets a bit sick of the same
old faces week after week - and

PAGE 52 and 53

squalid, and the surrounding country is flat and uninteresting. On the way, we visited Li Hung Chang's Memorial and also one or two Buddhist temples which were very interesting as we hadn't seen anything like them before. They were mostly filled with weird grotesque figures of the Bhudda, and most of the places were extremely dirty and dark. I forgot to mention that February 13th was the Chinese New Year, a festive season which they take very seriously, the festivities being spread over many days. The Chinese New Year does not always fall on the same date. Like our Easter, it is a moveable feast. A great concern of theirs at that time is that they should be able to pay off all their debts before the New Year, a very estimable desire! We were in Hong Kong on the Chinese New Year's Eve, and it was a very amusing sight because from every house in every street, they were continually setting light to firecrackers which went off with loud reports filling the streets with smoke. The object of all these explosions was to expel the Devils. All that I can say is that Devils must abound in China by the scores and thousands, because when we got to Shanghai, we could hardly sleep the first night for the noise of Devils still being expelled in the street below! I left Shanghai with many regrets on February 18th. I so enjoy being away from the rest of the passengers for a bit. One gets a bit sick of the same old faces week after week, and

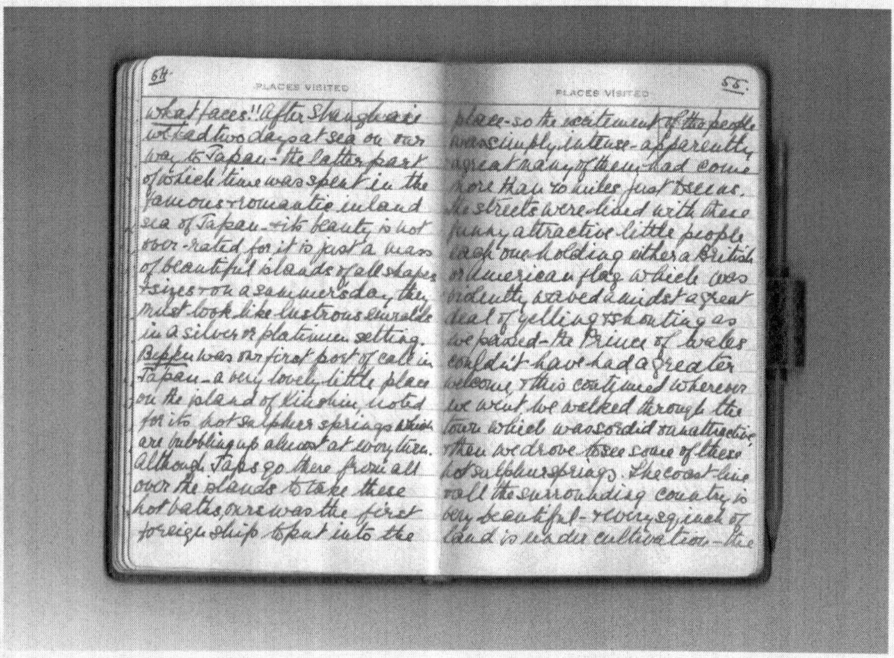

PAGE 54 and 55

what faces!! After Shanghai we had two days at sea on our way to Japan. The latter part of which time was spent in the famous and romantic inland Sea of Japan and its beauty is not overrated, for it is just a mass of beautiful islands of all shapes and sizes, and on a summer's day, they must look like lustrous emeralds in a silver or platinum setting. Beppu was our first port of call in Japan, a very lovely little place on the island of Kyushu, noted for its hot sulphur springs which are bubbling up almost at every turn. Although Japs go there from all over the islands to take these hot baths, ours was the first foreign ship to put into the place, so the excitement of the people was simply intense. Apparently, a great many of them had come more than 70 miles just to see us. The streets were lined with these funny attractive little people, each one holding either a British or American flag which was violently waved amidst a great deal of yelling and shouting as we passed. The Prince of Wales couldn't have had a greater welcome, and this continued wherever we went. We walked through the town which was sordid and unattractive, and then we drove to see some of these hot sulphur Springs. The coastline and all the surrounding country is very beautiful, and every square inch of land is under cultivation. The

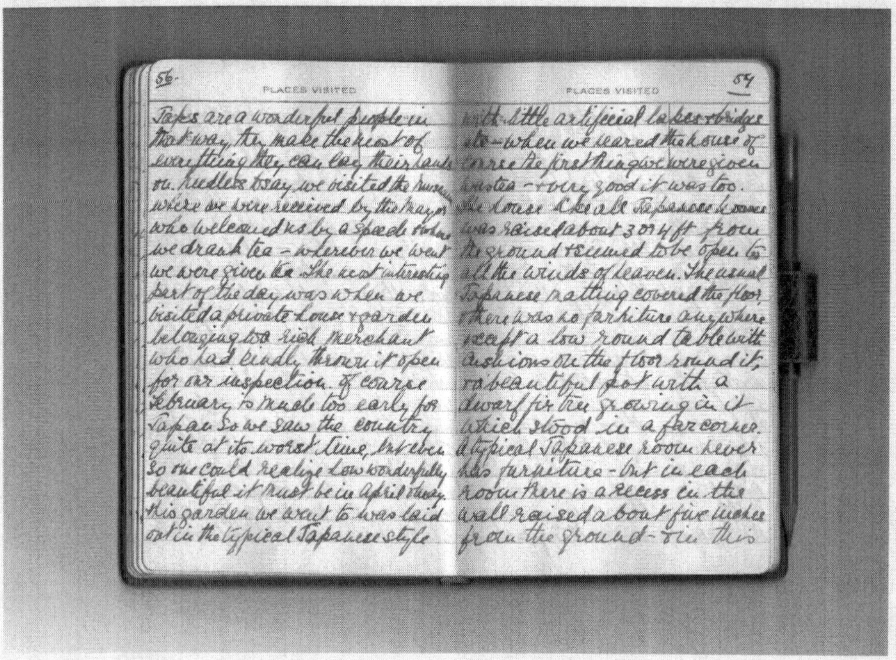

PAGE 56 and 57

Japs are a wonderful people in that way. They make the most of everything they can lay their hands on. Needless to say, we visited the museum where we were received by the Mayor who welcomed us by a speech and where we drank tea. Wherever we went, we were given tea. The most interesting part of thc day was when we visited a private house and garden belonging to a rich merchant who had kindly thrown it open for our inspection. Of course February is much too early for Japan, so we saw the country quite at its worst time, but even so one could realise how wonderfully beautiful it must be in April and May. This garden we went to was laid out in the typical Japanese style with little artificial lakes and bridges etc. When we neared the house of course, the first thing we were given was tea, and very good it was too. The house, like all Japanese houses, was raised about 3 or 4 feet from the ground, and seemed to be open to all the winds of heaven. The usual Japanese matting covered the floor, and there was no furniture anywhere except a low round table with cushions on the floor round it, and a beautiful pot with a dwarf fir tree growing in it which stood in a far corner. A typical Japanese room never has furniture, but in each room there is a recess in the wall raised about 5 inches from the ground, and in this

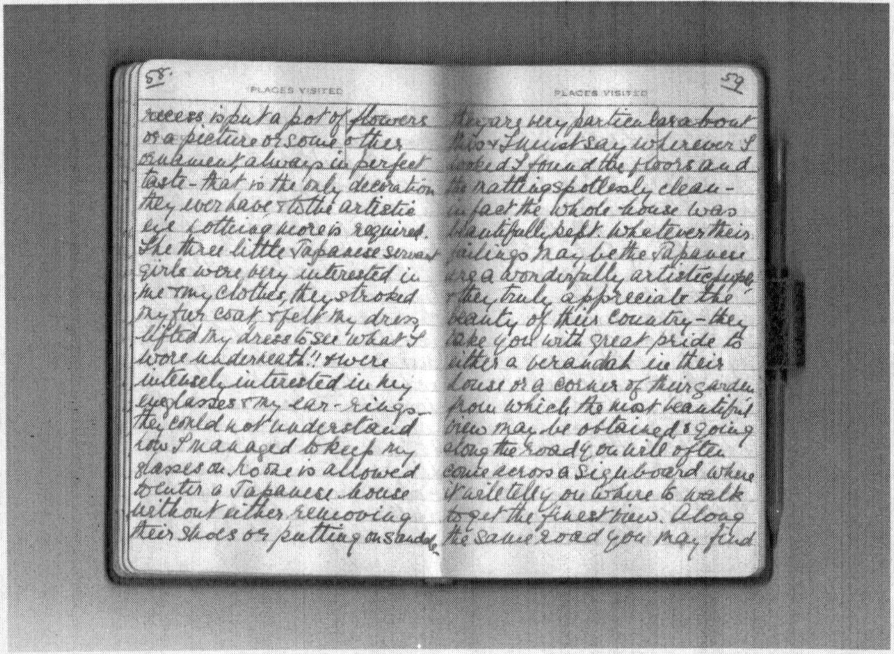

58.

PLACES VISITED

recess is put a pot of flowers
or a picture or some other
ornament, always in perfect
taste - that is the only decoration
they ever have & to the artistic
eye nothing more is required.
The three little Japanese servant
girls were very interested in
me & my clothes, they stroked
my fur coat & felt my dress
lifted my dress to see what I
wore underneath!! & were
intensely interested in my
eyeglasses & my ear-rings -
they could not understand
how I managed to keep my
glasses on. No one is allowed
to enter a Japanese house
without either removing
their shoes or putting on sandals

PLACES VISITED

59

they are very particular about
this & I must say wherever I
looked I found the floors and
the matting spotlessly clean -
in fact the whole house was
beautifully kept. Whatever their
failings may be the Japanese
are a wonderfully artistic people
& they truly appreciate the
beauty of their country - they
take you with great pride to
either a verandah in their
house or a corner of their garden
from which the most beautiful
view may be obtained & going
along the road you will often
come across a signboard where
it will tell you where to walk
to get the finest view. Along
the same road you may find

PAGE 58 and 59

recess is put a pot of flowers, or a picture or some other ornaments, always in perfect taste. That is the only decoration they ever have, and to the artistic eye, nothing more is required. The three little Japanese servant girls were very interested in me and my clothes. They stroked my fur coat and felt my dress. They lifted my dress to see what I wore underneath!!, and were intensely interested in my eyeglasses and my earrings. They could not understand how I managed to keep my glasses on. No one is allowed to enter a Japanese house without either removing their shoes or putting on sandals. They are very particular about this, and I must say wherever I looked, I found the floors and the matting spotlessly clean. In fact the whole house was beautifully kept. Whatever their failings may be, the Japanese are a wonderfully artistic people, and they truly appreciate the beauty of their country. They take you with great pride to either a verandah in their house or a corner of their garden from which the most beautiful view may be obtained, and going along the road, you will often come across a signboard where it will tell you where to walk to get the finest view. Along the same road you may find

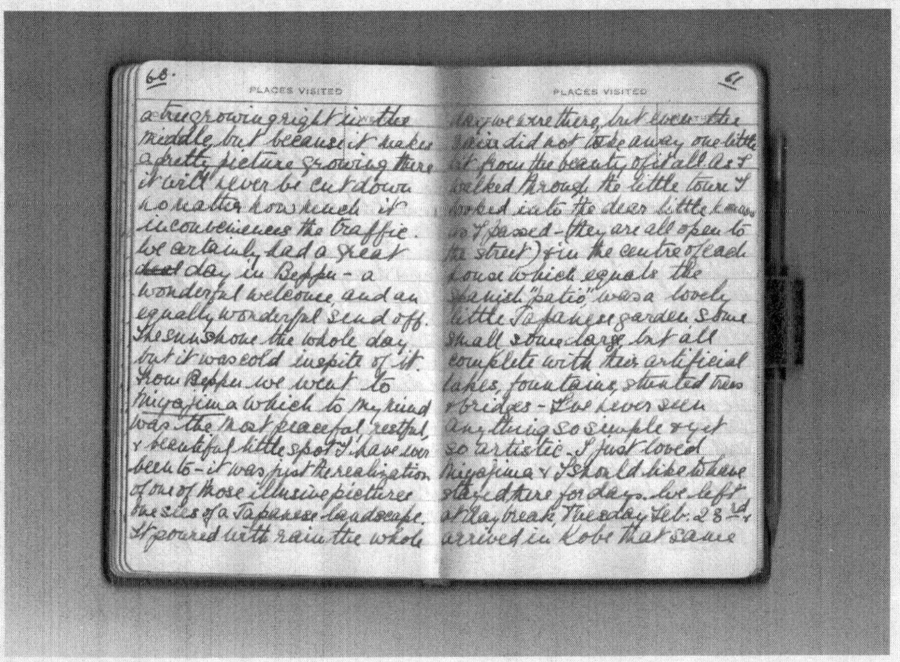

PAGE 60 and 61

a tree growing right in the middle, but because it makes a pretty picture growing there, it will never be cut down no matter how much it inconveniences the traffic. We certainly had a great day in Beppu, a wonderful welcome and an equally wonderful send off. The sun shone the whole day, but it was cold in spite of it. From Beppu, we went to Miyajima which to my mind was the most peaceful, restful, and beautiful little spot I have ever been to. It was just the realisation of one of those illusive pictures one sees of a Japanese landscape. It poured with rain the whole day we were there, but even the rain did not take away one little bit from the beauty of it all. As I walked through the little town, I looked into dear little houses as I passed. They are all open to the street, and in the centre of each house, which equals the Spanish "patio", was a lovely little Japanese garden. Some small, some large, but all complete with their artificial lakes, fountains, stunted trees and bridges. I've never seen anything so simple and yet so artistic. I just loved Miyajima, and I should like to have stayed there for days. We left at daybreak on Tuesday, February 23rd, and arrived in Kobe that same

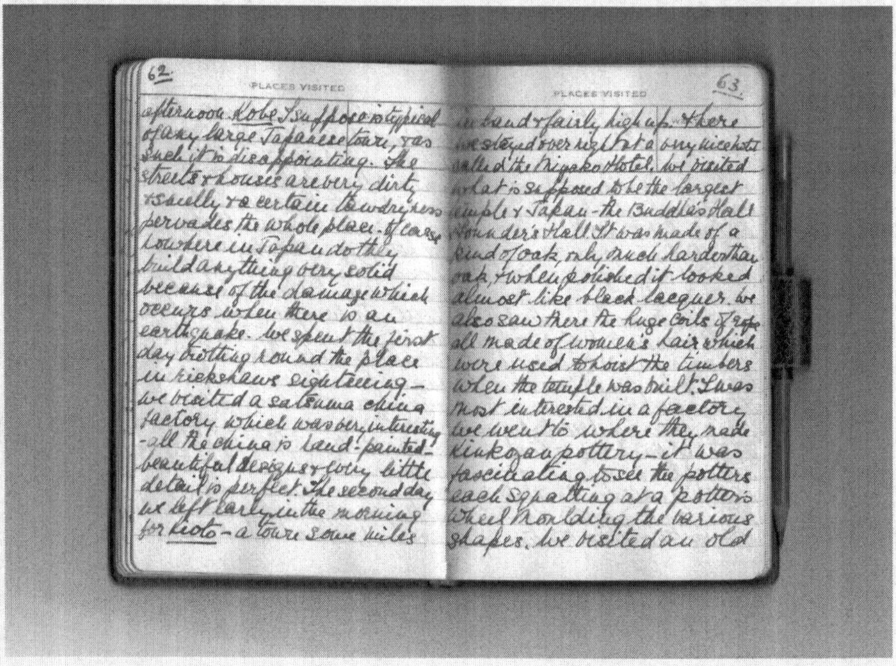

PAGE 62 and 63

afternoon. Kobe I suppose is typical of any large Japanese town, and as such it is disappointing. The streets and houses are very dirty and smelly, and a certain tawdriness pervades the whole place. Of course, nowhere in Japan do they build anything very solid because of the damage which occurs when there is an earthquake. We spent the first day trotting round the place in rick-shaws sightseeing. We visited a Satsuma china factory which was very inter-esting. All the china is hand painted with beautiful designs, and every little detail is perfect. The second day we left early in the morning for Kioto, a town some miles inland and fairly high up. There we stayed overnight at a very nice hotel called the Miyako Hotel. We visited what is supposed to be the largest temple in Japan, the Buddha's Hall and Founder's Hall. It was made of a kind of oak, only much harder than oak, and when polished, it looked almost like black lacquer. We also saw there the huge coils of rope, all made of women's hair which were used to hoist the timbers when the temple was built. I was most interested in a factory we went to where they made Kinkozan pottery. It was fascinating to see the potters each squatting at a potter's wheel moulding the various shapes. We visited an old

Hong Kong Harbour in 1925 (page 42 & 43 in the diary)

Repulse Bay Hotel in 1925 (page 48 & 49 in the diary)

Kinkozan Pottery (page 62 & 63 in the diary

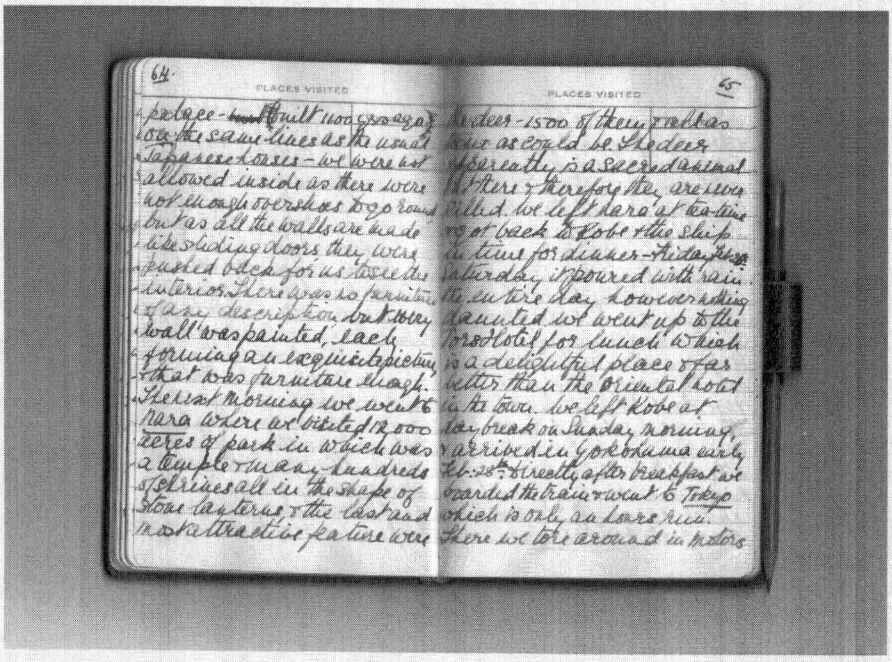

PAGE 64 and 65

palace built 1100 years ago on the same lines as the usual Japanese houses. We were not allowed inside as there were not enough overshoes to go round, but as all the walls are made like sliding doors, they were pushed back for us to see the interior. There was no furniture of any description, but every wall was painted, each forming an exquisite picture and that was furniture enough. The next morning we went to Nara where we visited 12,000 acres of park in which was a temple and many hundreds of shrines, all in the shape of stone lanterns, and the last and most attractive feature were the deer, 1500 of them, and all as tame as could be. The deer apparently is a sacred animal and therefore they are never killed. We left Nara at teatime, and got back to Kobe and the ship in time for dinner. On Friday, February 26th, a Saturday, it poured with rain the entire day, however nothing daunted, we went up to the Tors Hotel for lunch which is a delightful place and far better than the Oriental Hotel in the town. We left Kobe at daybreak on Sunday morning, and arrived in Yokohama early on February 28th. Directly after breakfast, we boarded the train and went to Tokyo which is only an hour's run. There we tore around in motors

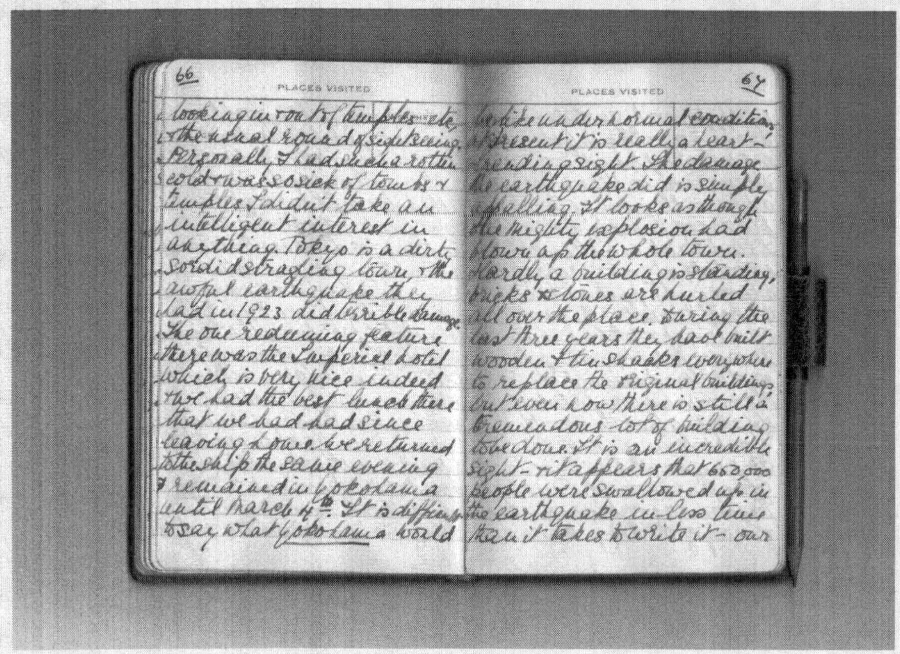

PAGE 66 and 67

looking in and out of temples etc, and the usual round of sightseeing. Personally, I had such a rotten cold and was so sick of tombs and temples, I didn't take an intelligent interest in anything. Tokyo is a dirty sordid straggling town, and the awful earthquake they had in 1923 did terrible damage. The one redeeming feature there was the Imperial Hotel which is very nice indeed, and we had the best lunch there that we had had since leaving home. We returned to the ship the same evening and remained in Yokohama until March 4th. It is difficult to say what Yokohama would be like under normal conditions. At present it is really a heartrending sight. The damage the earthquake did is simply appalling. It looks as though one mighty explosion had blown up the whole town. Hardly a building is standing. Bricks and stones are hurled all over the place. During the last three years, they have built wooden and tin shacks everywhere to replace the original buildings, but even now, there is still a tremendous lot of building to be done. It is an incredible sight, and it appears that 650,000 were swallowed up in the earthquake in less time than it takes to write about it. Our

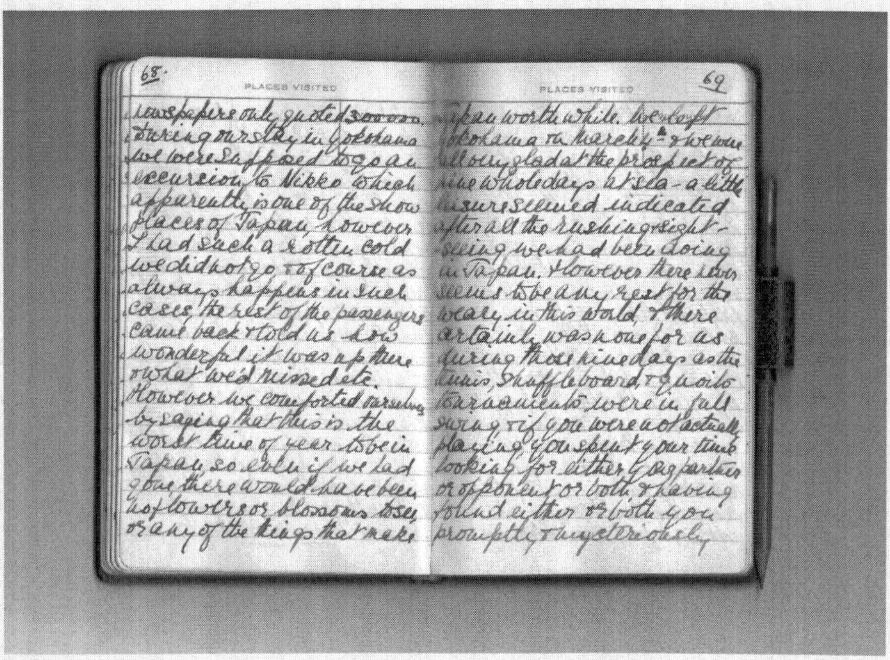
68.
PLACES VISITED
newspapers only quoted 300000.
During our stay in Yokohama
we were supposed to go on
excursion to Nikko which
apparently is one of the show
places of Japan, however
I had such a rotten cold
we did not go & of course as
always happens in such
cases, the rest of the passengers
came back & told us how
wonderful it was up there
& what we'd missed etc.
However we comforted ourselves
by saying that this is the
worst time of year to be in
Japan, so even if we had
gone there would have been
no flowers or blossoms to see,
or any of the things that make

69
PLACES VISITED
Japan worth while. We left
Yokohama on March 4th & we were
all very glad at the prospect of
nine whole days at sea - a little
leisure seemed indicated
after all the rushing & sight-
seeing we had been doing
in Japan. However there never
seems to be any rest for the
weary in this world, & there
certainly was none for us
during those nine days as the
tennis, shuffleboard, & quoits
tournaments were in full
swing, & if you were not actually
playing you spent your time
looking for either your partner
or opponent or both, & having
found either or both you
promptly & mysteriously

PAGE 68 and 69

newspapers only quoted 300,000. During our stay in Yokohama, we were supposed to go on an excursion to Nikko which apparently is one of the show places of Japan, however I had such a rotten cold, we did not go, and of course, as always happens in such cases, the rest of the passengers came back and told us how wonderful it was up there, and what we'd missed etc. However, we comforted ourselves by saying that this is the worst time of year to be in Japan, so even if we had gone, there would have been no flowers or blossoms to see, or any of the things that make Japan worthwhile. We left Yokohama on March 4th, and we were all very glad at the prospect of nine whole days at sea. A little leisure seemed indicated after all the rushing and sightseeing we had been doing in Japan. However, there never seems to be any rest for the weary in this world, and there certainly was none for us during those nine days as the tennis, shuffleboard and quoits tournaments were in full swing, and if you were not actually playing, you spent your time looking for either your partner or opponent or both, and having found either or both, you promptly and mysteriously

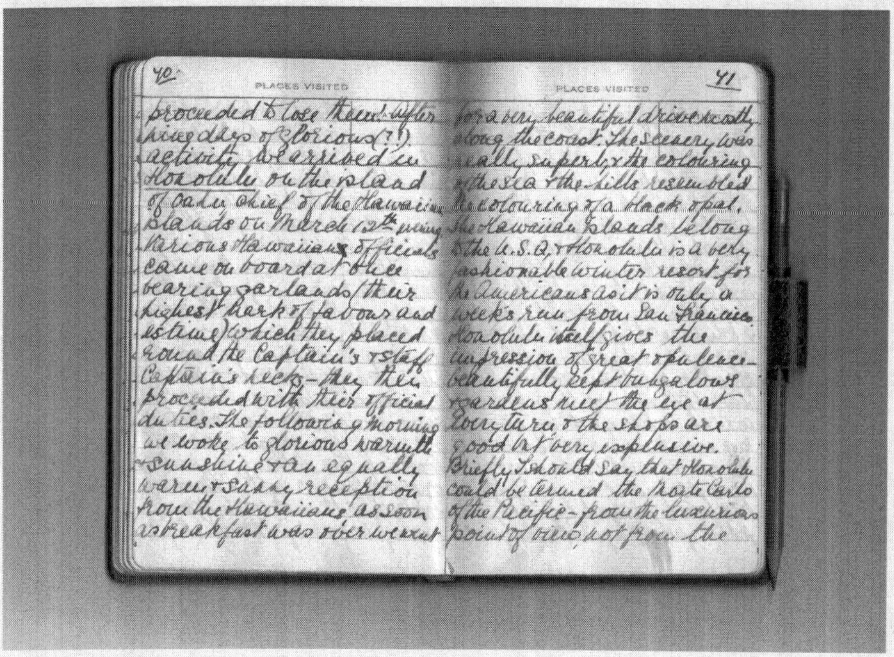

PAGE 70 and 71

proceeded to lose them! After nine days of glorious(??) activity, we arrived in Honolulu on the island of Oahu, chief of the Hawaiian Islands on March 12th in the evening. Various Hawaiian officials came on board at once bearing garlands, (their highest mark of favour and esteem), which they placed round the captain's and staff captain's necks. They then proceeded with their official duties. The following morning we woke to glorious warmth and sunshine, and an equally warm and sunny reception from the Hawaiians. As soon as breakfast was over, we went for a very beautiful drive mostly along the coast. The scenery was really superb, and the colouring of the sea and the hills resemble the colouring of a black opal. The Hawaiin Islands belong to the USA, and Honolulu is a very fashionable winter resort for the Americans as it is only a week's run from San Francisco. Honolulu itself gives the impression of great opulence, beautifully kept bungalows and gardens meet the eye at every turn, and the shops are good but very expensive. Briefly, I should say that Honolulu could be termed the Monte Carlo of the Pacific from the luxurious point of view, not from the

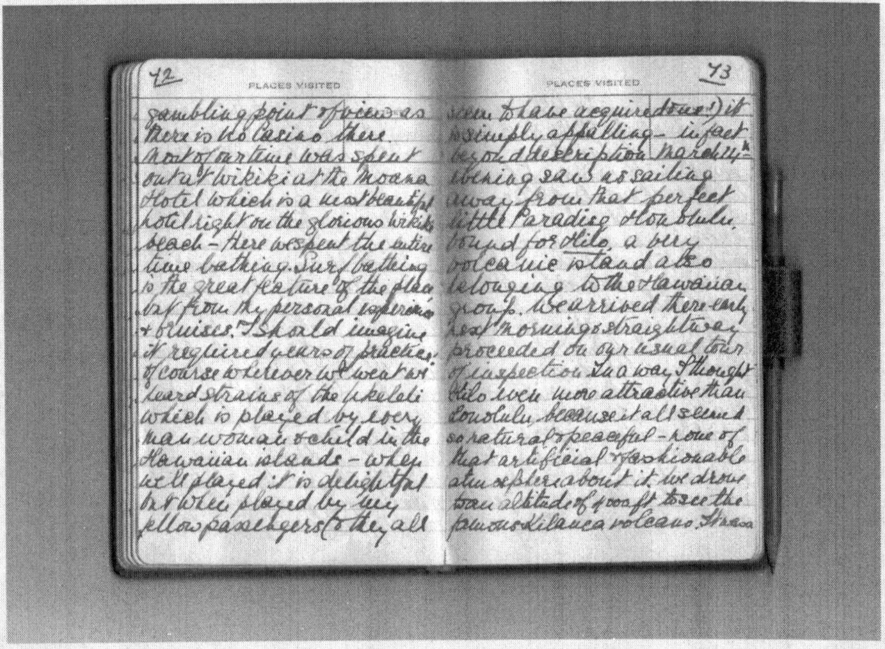

PAGE 72 and 73

gambling point of view as there is no casino there. Most of our time was spent out at Waikiki at the Moana Hotel which is the most beautiful hotel right on the glorious Waikiki beach. There we spent the entire time bathing. Surf bathing is the great feature of the place, but from my personal experience and bruises, I should imagine it requires years of practice. Of course wherever we went we heard strains of the ukelele which is played by every man, woman and child in the Hawaiian Islands. When well played it is delightful, but when played by my fellow passengers, (and they all seem to have acquired one), it is simply appalling - in fact beyond description. March 14th evening saw us sailing away from that perfect little paradise, Honolulu, bound for Hilo, a very volcanic island also belonging to the Hawaiian group. We arrived there early next morning, and straightaway proceeded on our usual tour of inspection. In a way, I thought Hilo even more attractive than Honolulu because it all seemed so natural and peaceful. None of that artificial and fashionable atmosphere about it. We drove to an altitude of 4000 feet to see the famous Kilauea Volcano. It was a

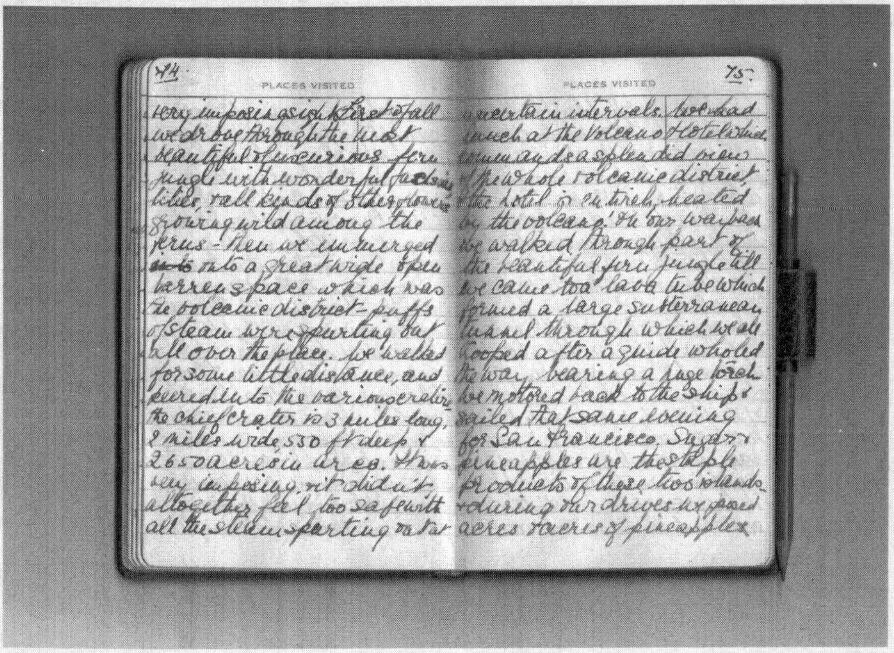

PAGE 74 and 75

very imposing sight. First of all we drove through the most beautiful and luxurious fern jungle with wonderful fuchsias, lilies and all kinds of other flowers growing wild among the ferns. Then we emerged onto a great wide open barren space which was the volcanic district. Puffs of steam were spurting out all over the place. We walked for some little distance, and peered into the various craters. The chief crater is 3 miles long, 2 miles wide, 550 feet deep and 2650 acres in area. It was very imposing, and it didn't altogether feel too safe with all the steam spurting out at uncertain intervals. We had lunch at the Volcano Hotel which commands a splendid view of the whole volcanic district. The hotel is entirely heated by the volcano! On our way back, we walked through part of the beautiful fern jungle until we came to a lava tube which formed a large subterranean tunnel through which we all trooped after a guide who led the way bearing a huge torch. We motored back to the ship, and sailed that same evening for San Francisco. Sugar and pineapples are the staple products of these two islands, and during our drives, we passed acres and acres of pineapple

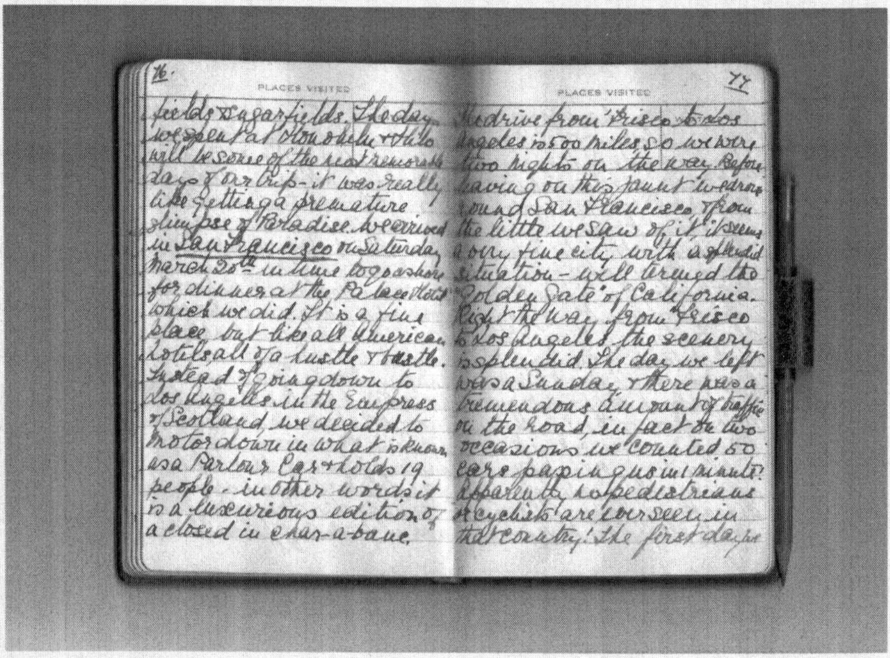

PAGE 76 and 77

fields and sugar fields. The days we spent at Honolulu and Hilo will be some of the most memorable days of our trip. It was really like getting a premature glimpse of paradise. We arrived in San Francisco on Saturday March 20th, in time to go ashore for dinner at the Palace Hotel which we did. It is a fine place, but like all American hotels, all of a hustle and bustle. Instead of going down to Los Angeles in the Empress of Scotland, we decided to motor down in what is known as a Parlour Car, and holds 19 people. In other words, it is a luxurious edition of a closed in charabanc. The drive from 'Frisco to Los Angeles is 500 miles, so we were two nights on the way. Before leaving on this jaunt, we drove round San Francisco, and from the little we saw of it, it seems a very fine city with a splendid situation, well termed "The Golden Gate" of California. Right the way from 'Frisco to Los Angeles the scenery is splendid. The day we left was a Sunday, and there was a tremendous amount of traffic on the road, in fact on two occasions we counted 50 cars passing us in one minute! Apparently no pedestrians or cyclists are ever seen in that country! The first day we

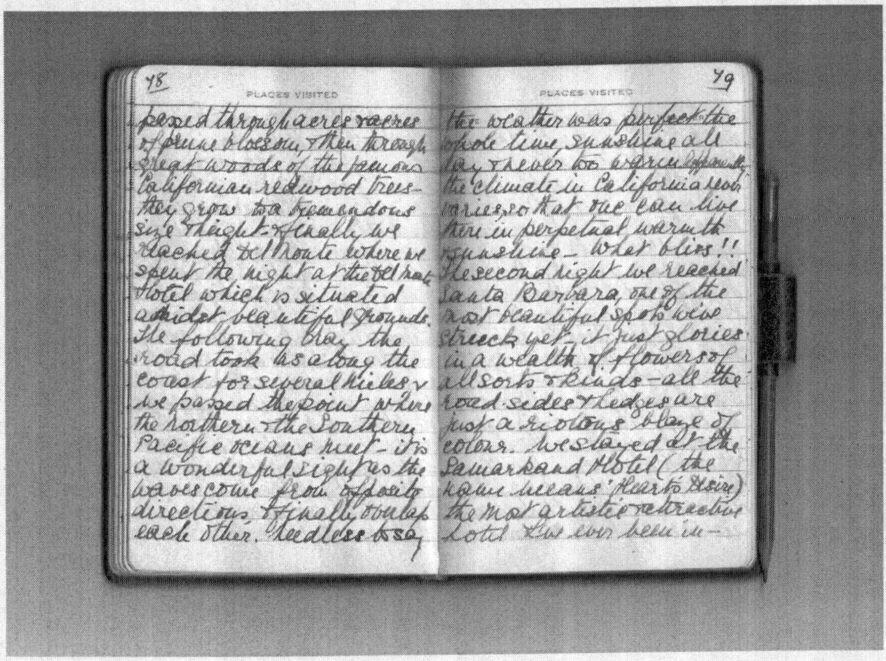

PAGE 78 and 79

passed through acres and acres of prune blossom, and then through great woods of the famous Californian redwood trees. They grow to a tremendous size and height. Finally, we reached Del Monte where we spent the night at the Del Monte Hotel which is situated amidst the beautiful grounds. The following day, the road took us along the coast for several miles, and we passed the point where the Northern and the Southern Pacific Oceans meet. It is a wonderful sight as the waves come from opposite directions, and finally overlap each other. Needless to say, the weather was perfect the whole time. Sunshine all day and never too warm. Apparently the climate in California never varies, so that one can live there in perpetual warmth and sunshine - what bliss!! The second night we reached Santa Barbara, one of the most beautiful spots we've struck yet. It just glories in a wealth of flowers of all sorts and kinds. All the roadsides and hedges are just a riotous blaze of colour. We stayed at the Samarkand Hotel, (the name means "Hearts Desire"), the most artistic and attractive hotel I've ever been in.

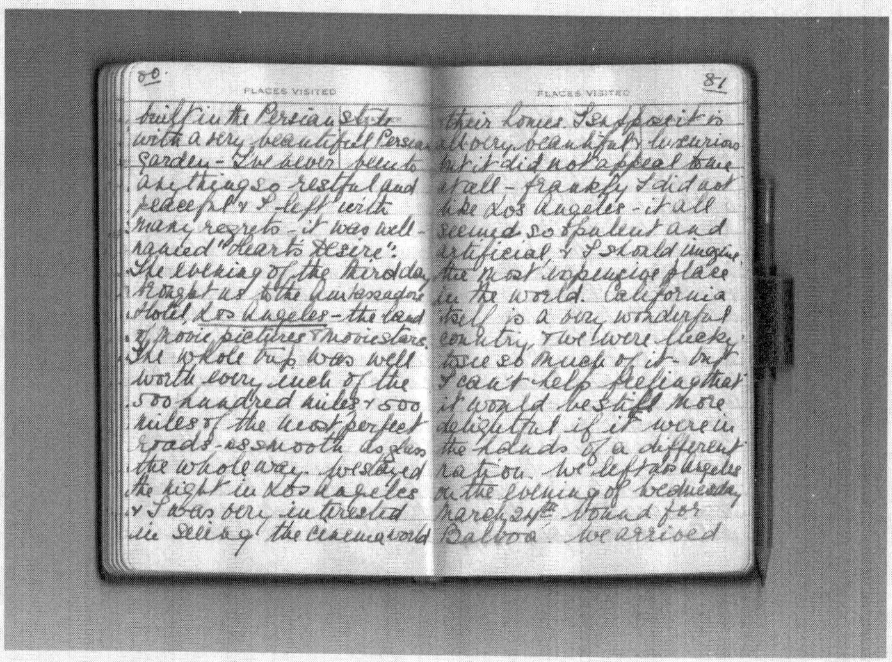
80

PLACES VISITED

built in the Persian style
with a very beautiful Persian
garden - I've never been to
anything so restful and
peaceful & I left with
many regrets - it was well-
named "Hearts Desire".
The evening of the third day
brought us to the Ambassadors
Hotel, Los Angeles - the land
of movie pictures & movie stars.
The whole trip was well
worth every inch of the
500 hundred miles & 500
miles of the most perfect
roads - as smooth as glass
the whole way. We stayed
the night in Los Angeles
& I was very interested
in seeing the cinema world

81

PLACES VISITED

their homes. I suppose it is
all very beautiful & luxurious
but it did not appeal to me
at all - frankly I did not
like Los Angeles - it all
seemed so opulent and
artificial, & I should imagine
the most expensive place
in the world. California
itself is a very wonderful
country, & we were lucky
to see so much of it - but
I can't help feeling that
it would be still more
delightful if it were in
the hands of a different
nation. We left Los Angeles
on the evening of Wednesday
March 24th bound for
Balboa. We arrived

PAGE 80 and 81

It is built in the Persian style with a very beautiful Persian garden. I've never been to anything so restful and peaceful, and I left with many regrets. It was well named "Hearts Desire". The evening of the third day brought us to the Ambassador Hotel, Los Angeles, the land of movie pictures and movie stars. The whole trip was well worth every inch of the 500 miles, and 500 miles of the most perfect roads, as smooth as glass the whole way. We stayed the night in Los Angeles, and I was very interested in seeing the cinema world and their homes. I suppose it is all very beautiful and luxurious, but it did not appeal to me at all. Frankly, I did not like Los Angeles. It all seemed so opulent and artificial, and I should imagine the most expensive place in the world. California itself is a very wonderful country, and we were lucky to see so much of it, but I can't help feeling that it would be still more delightful if it were in the hands of a different nation. We left Los Angeles on the evening of Wednesday, March 24th, bound for Balboa. We arrived

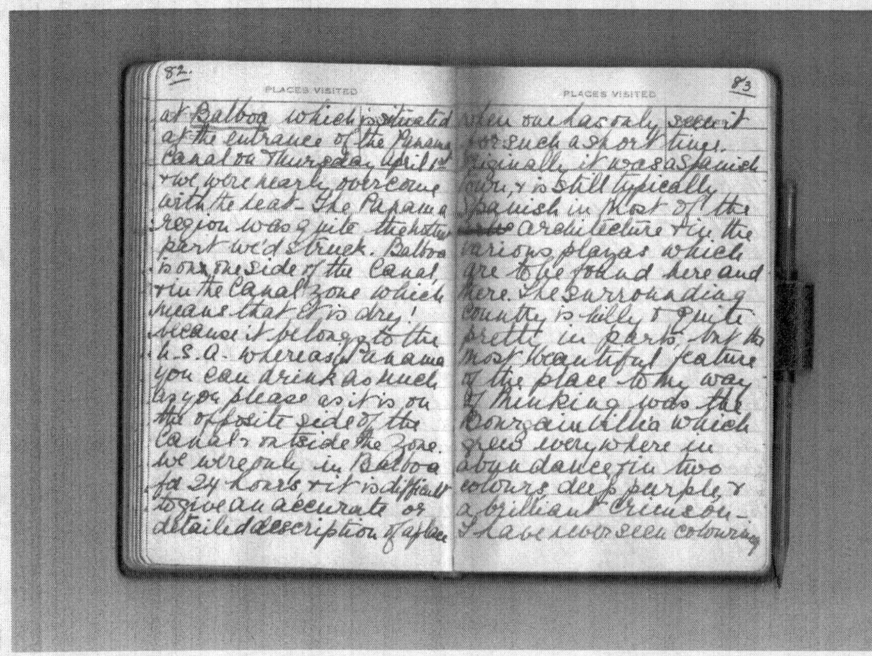

PAGE 82 and 83

at Balboa, which is situated at the entrance of the Panama Canal, on Thursday, April 1st, and we were nearly overcome with the heat. The Panama region was quite the hottest part we'd struck. Balboa is on one side of the canal and in the Canal zone which means that it is dry! because it belongs to the USA, whereas in Panama you can drink as much as you please, as it is on the opposite side of the canal and outside the zone. We were only in Balboa for 24 hours, and it is difficult to give an accurate or detailed description of a place when one has only seen it for such a short time. Originally it was a Spanish town, and is still typically Spanish in most of the architecture, and in the various plazas which are to be found here and there. The surrounding country is hilly and quite pretty in parts, but the most beautiful feature of the place to my way of thinking was the bougainvillea which grew everywhere in abundance, and in two colours, deep purple and a brilliant crimson. I have never seen colouring

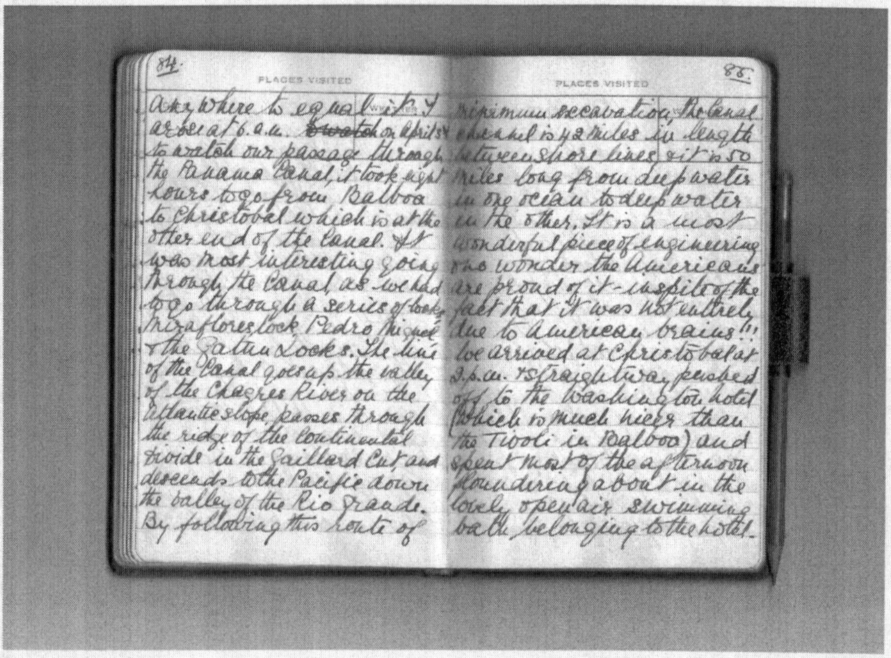

PAGE 84 and 85

anywhere to equal it. I rose at 6 am on April 3rd to watch our passage through the Panama Canal. It took eight hours to go from Balboa to Cristobal which is at the other end of the canal. It was most interesting going through the canal, as we had to go through a series of locks. Miraflores Lock, Pedro Miguel and the Gatun locks. The line of the canal goes up the valley of the Chargres River on the Atlantic slope. it passes through the ridge of the Continental divide in the Gaillard Cut, and descends to the Pacific down the valley of the Rio Grande. By following this route of minimum excavation, the canal channel is 42 miles in length between shorelines and it is 50 miles long from deep water in one ocean to deep water in the other. It is a most wonderful piece of engineering, and no wonder the Americans are proud of it, in spite of the fact that it was not entirely due to the American brains!! We arrived at Cristobal at 2 pm, and straight away pushed off to the Washington Hotel, (which is much nicer than the Tivoli in Balboa), and spent most of the afternoon floundering about in the lovely open-air swimming bath belonging to the hotel.

The Moana Hotel (page 72 & 73 in the diary)

The Gatun Locks (page 84 & 85 in the diary)

The Pedro Miguel Lock (page 84 & 85 in the diary)

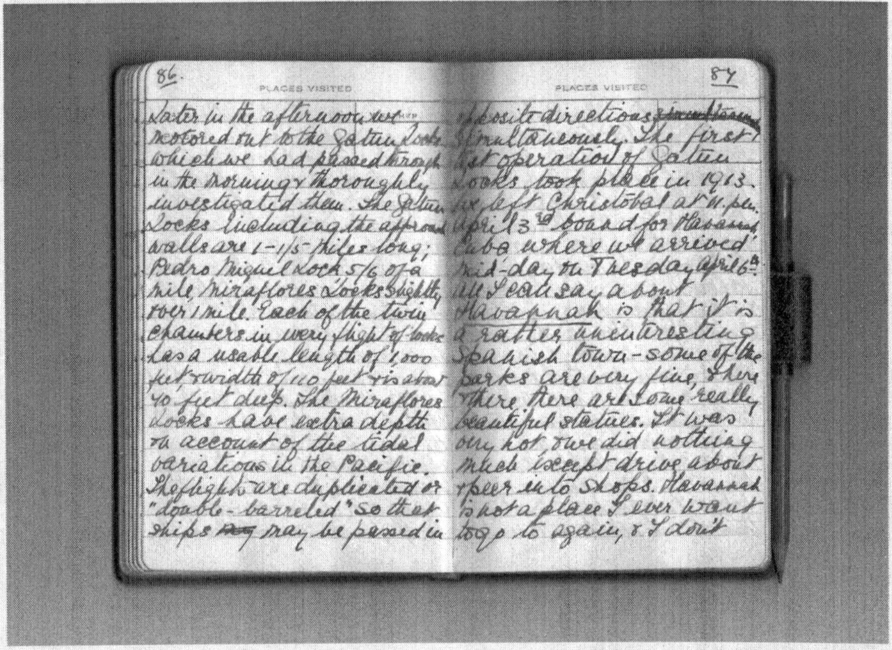
86.
PLACES VISITED
Later in the afternoon we
motored out to the Gatun Locks
which we had passed through
in the morning & thoroughly
investigated them. The Gatun
Locks including the approach
walls are 1-1/5 miles long;
Pedro Miguel Lock 5/6 of a
mile Miraflores Locks slightly
over 1 mile. Each of the twin
chambers in every flight of locks
has a usable length of 1000
feet & width of 110 feet & is about
70 feet deep. The Miraflores
Locks have extra depth
on account of the tidal
variations in the Pacific.
The flights are duplicated or
"double-barreled" so that
ships ~~may~~ may be passed in

87
PLACES VISITED
opposite directions ~~simultaneously~~
simultaneously. The first
test operation of Gatun
Locks took place in 1913.
We left Cristobal at 11 pm.
April 3rd bound for Havana
Cuba where we arrived
mid-day on Tuesday April 6th.
All I can say about
Havannah is that it is
a rather uninteresting
Spanish town - some of the
parks are very fine, & here
& there there are some really
beautiful statues. It was
very hot, & we did nothing
much except drive about
& peer into shops. Havannah
is not a place I ever want
to go to again, & I don't

PAGE 86 and 87

Later in the afternoon, we motored out to the Gatun locks which we had passed through in the morning and thoroughly investigated them. The Gatun locks, including the approach walls, are one to one and a half miles long. Pedro Miguel Lock, 5/6ths of a mile, Miraflores locks, slightly over 1 mile. Each of the twin chambers in every flight of locks has a usable length of 1000 feet and width of 110 feet, and is about 70 feet deep. The Miraflores locks have extra depth on account of the tidal variations in the Pacific. The flights are duplicated or double barrelled, so that ships may be passed in opposite directions simultaneously. The first test operation of Gatun locks took place in 1913. We left Cristobal at 11 pm on April 3rd bound for Havana, Cuba where we arrived midday on Tuesday, April 6th. All I can say about Havana is that it is a rather uninteresting Spanish town. Some of the parks are very fine. Here and there, there are some really beautiful statues. It was very hot, and we did nothing much except drive about and peer into the shops. Havana is not a place I ever want to go to again, and I don't

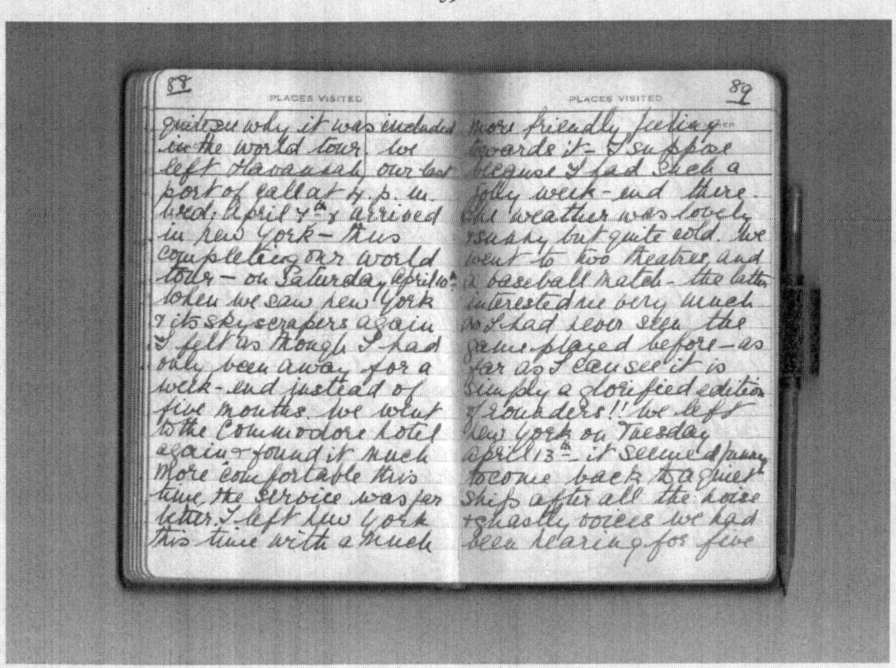

PAGE 88 and 89

quite see why it was included in the world tour. We left Havana, our last port of call at 4 pm on Wednesday, April 7th, and arrived in New York, thus completing our World Tour. On Saturday, April 10th, when we saw New York and its skyscrapers again, I felt as though I had only been away for a weekend instead of five months. We went to the Commodore Hotel again and found it much more comfortable this time. The service was far better. I left New York this time with a much more friendly feeling towards it, I suppose because I had such a jolly weekend there. The weather was lovely and sunny but quite cold. We went to two theatres and a baseball match. The latter interested me very much as I had never seen the game played before. As far as I can see, it is simply a glorified edition of rounders!! We left New York on Tuesday, April 13th. It seemed funny to come back to a quiet ship after all the noise and ghastly voices we had been hearing for five

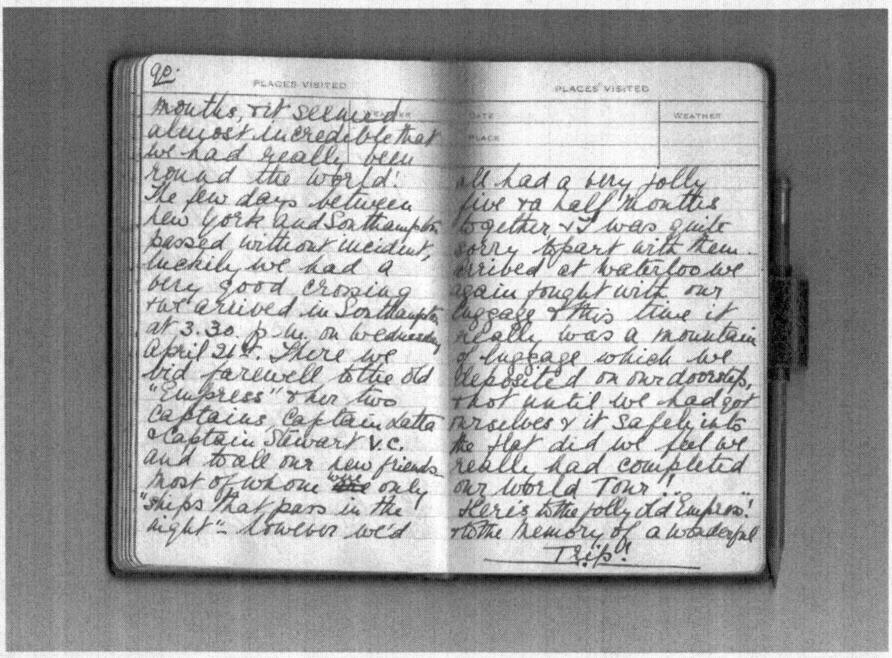
90.
PLACES VISITED
months, & it seemed
almost incredible that
we had really been
round the world!
The few days between
New York and Southampton
passed without incident,
luckily we had a
very good crossing
& we arrived in Southampton
at 3.30. p.m. on Wednesday
April 21st. There we
bid farewell to the old
"Empress" & her two
captains, Captain Latta
& Captain Stewart V.C.
and to all our new friends
most of whom were only
"ships that pass in the
night" - however we'd

PLACES VISITED
DATE
WEATHER
PLACE
all had a very jolly
five & a half months
together & I was quite
sorry to part with them.
arrived at Waterloo we
again fought with our
luggage & this time it
really was a mountain
of luggage which we
deposited on our doorstep,
& not until we had got
ourselves & it safely into
the flat did we feel we
really had completed
our World Tour! ...
Here's to the jolly old Empress!
& to the memory of a wonderful
Trip!

PAGE 90 and 91

months, and it seemed almost incredible that we had really been round the world! The few days between New York and Southampton passed without incident. Luckily we had a very good crossing, and we arrived in Southampton at 3:30 pm on Wednesday, April 21st. There we bid farewell to the old "Empress" and her two captains, captain Latta and captain Stewart V.C. and to all our new friends, most of whom were only 'ships that pass in the night'!. However, we'd all had a very jolly five and a half months together, and I was quite sorry to part with them. We arrived at Waterloo and again fought with our luggage, and this time it really was a mountain of luggage which we deposited on our doorstep. Not until we had got ourselves and it safely into the flat did we feel we really had completed our World Tour!
Here's to the jolly old "Empress"! and to the memory of a wonderful trip!